THE EATIN

"...an opinionated little compendium."
~ New York Times

"...irresistible little guide."
~ Chicago Tribune

"an elegant, small guide..."
~ Minneapolis Star Tribune

"Makes dining easy and enjoyable."
~ Toronto Sun

""...a terrific primer for first-time visitors."
~ Houston Chronicle

""...opening up the world of good eating with their innovative paperback series."
~ Salt Lake Tribune

"It's written as if a friend were talking to you."
~ Celebrity Chef Tyler Florence

"...travelers who know their cervelle *(brains) from* cervelle de canut *(herbed cheese spread)."*
~ USA Today

"Order like an Italian."
~ Boston Globe

•

ABOUT THE AUTHORS

Andy Herbach is the author of *Eating & Drinking in Paris*, *Eating & Drinking in Spain and Portugal* and *Eating & Drinking in Latin America*.

He is also the author of several books published by Europe Made Easy Travel Guides, including *Paris Walks*, *Europe Made Easy*, *Paris Made Easy*, *Berlin Made Easy*, *Amsterdam Made Easy*, *French Riviera Made Easy*, *Oslo Made Easy*, *Barcelona Made Easy*, and *Italy Made Easy*.

Earlier editions of this book were written with Michael Dillon. All illustrations are by Michael Dillon.

You can e-mail comments, additions and corrections to eatndrink@aol.com.

You can visit our website at www.eatndrink.com.

ACKNOWLEDGMENTS

Marian Olson (our Miss Know-It-All English editor) and Angelina Bellotti (our Italian editor) were of great help in the original edition of this book. Thanks also to Jonathan Stein, our Open Road publisher.

Special thanks to those who have helped us find the restaurants in this guide, especially Mark Berry and Dan Schmidt who suffered through many meals and countless bottles of wine on our behalf.

This ninth edition was updated by Andy Herbach. Andy thanks Karl Raaum for all his help.

EATING AND DRINKING IN

Italian

Andy Herbach

EUROPE MADE EASY TRAVEL GUIDES

Europe Made Easy
Travel Guides

www.eatndrink.com

Ninth Edition
Earlier editions of this book were under the title
Eating & Drinking in Italy.

Table of Contents

Introduction

Can you imagine a foreign traveler who speaks basic English understanding what prime rib is? Or a porterhouse? Veggie platter, anyone? Buffalo wings? Sloppy joes?

Even people who speak passable Italian can have trouble reading a menu. You may know *ricotta* cheese, but not *malfatti di ricotta* which means "badly made," a reference to the handmade dumpling with *ricotta* cheese filling. You may be surprised to find *puttanesca* (which means *in the style of a prostitute*) on the menu. It's a sauce of tomatoes, capers, anchovies, black olives and garlic.

Understanding the customs and food of a country helps travelers understand the people who live in the country.

If you love to travel as we do, you know the importance of a good guide. The same is true of dining. A good guide can make all the difference between a memorable evening and a dizzyingly bad one. This guide will help you find your way around a menu written in Italian. It gives you the freedom to enter places you might never have before and order a dinner without shouting, pointing and hand waving. Instead of fumbling with a bulky, conspicuous tourist guide (most of which usually include a very incomplete listing of foods) in a restaurant, this book is a pocket-sized alphabetical listing of food and drink commonly found on menus in Italy.

Although, now that we think about it, a dinner without shouting and hand waving is not truly Italian.

Of course, traveling to a foreign country means something different to everyone. For every vacation there are different expectations, different needs, and every traveler has his or her own idea of what will make that vacation memorable. For us, the making of a memorable vacation begins and ends with food.

We spent the morning staring at the Sistine Chapel and the Vatican Museum, but what stands out in our minds is the wonderful lunch in the *trattoria* afterward. The creamy shrimp pasta dish was as heavenly as Michelangelo's masterpiece. We spent a morning driving to see the Leaning Tower of Pisa, but the grilled lamb in Lerici made the day.

We know the panic of opening a menu without recognizing one word on it and the disappointment of being served something other than what you thought you'd ordered. On our first trip to Europe, we were served a plate of cold brains; we thought we had ordered chicken. This guide was created for the traveler who wants to enjoy, appreciate and experience authentic cuisine *and* know what he or she is eating.

The next time you find yourself seated in a red-tiled courtyard with the scent of simmering garlic in the night air and an incomprehensible menu in your hands, simply pull this guide from your pocket and get ready to enjoy the delicious cuisine of Italy.

In Italy and Ticino (the Italian-speaking region of Switzerland), the menu is almost always posted outside of the restaurant or in a window. This makes choosing a restaurant easy and fun as you "window shop" for your next meal.

Remember that the dish that you ordered may not be exactly as described in this guide. Every chef is (and should be) innovative. What we have listed for you in this guide is the most common version of a dish.

If a menu has an English translation it does not mean that the translation is correct.

In Italy, it's customary to order a first course (pasta, rice or soup), a second course (meat, poultry or fish) and a side dish (salad, potato or vegetable). Rarely does an Italian order only a first course (such as ordering only pasta), but that doesn't mean you can't.

Tipping

A service charge is almost always added to your bill (*il conto*) in Italy. Depending on the service, it's sometimes appropriate to leave up to 5%. Most locals round up to the next euro and it's okay if that is what you do, too. Travelers from the U.S. sometimes have trouble *not* tipping. Remember, you do *not* have to tip. The menu will usually note that service is included (***servizio incluso*** or ***servizio compreso***).

You will often find ***coperto*** or cover charge on your menu (a charge just for placing your butt at the table). This flat fee is usually between one euro to three euros per person.

Mealtimes

In northern Italy, lunch is served from noon to around 2 p.m., and dinner from 7 p.m. to 10 p.m. In the south, lunch is served from 1 p.m. and dinner from 8 p.m. No "early bird special" in Italy. Ticino's hours are the same as in northern Italy.

Water

Europeans joke that you can tell a U.S. tourist from his fanny pack, clothes and ubiquitous bottle of mineral water. Tap water is safe in Italy and Switzerland. Occasionally, you will find *non potabile* signs in rest rooms (especially in the rest stops of highways). This means that the water is not safe for drinking.

Waiters and waitresses will often bring *acqua minerale* (mineral water) to your table. You will be charged for it, so if you do not want mineral water ask for *acqua semplice* or *acqua di rubinetto* (tap water).

Restaurants in This Guide

Each of our recommended restaurants offers something different. Some have great food and little ambiance. Others have great ambiance and adequate food. Still others have both. Our goal is to find restaurants that are moderately priced and enjoyable. All restaurants have been tried and tested. Not enough can be said for a friendly welcome and great service. No matter how fabulous the meal, the experience will always be better when the staff treats you as if they actually want you there rather than simply tolerating your presence.

Times can change and restaurants can close, so do a walk-by earlier in the day or the day before, if possible. Our full list of restaurants starting on page 99 includes many of the eating establishments listed below.

Types of Eating Establishments

Bacaro: Venetian wine bar serving snacks like Spanish *tapas.*
Bar: Bars serve espresso, cappuccino, rolls, small sandwiches, alcoholic beverages and soft drinks.
Bottiglieria: Simple drinking establishments with limited menus but plenty of bottles of wine. Originally, these "bottle shops" served only liquor. Also called *fiaschetteria, cantina* or *trani.*
Enoteca: Wine bar.
Gelateria: Shop serving *gelato* (ice cream).
Grotta: Ticino has many *grotte*. These are village restaurants that take their name from caves used to store food and wine. Originally, a *grotta* was a simple eating establishment, but today many are quite expensive with extensive menus.
Locanda: Found in the country, serves regional meats and seafood.

Osteria: A tavern or wine shop. This name has also come to refer to a restaurant. These can also be called *cucina* or *hostaria*.

Paninoteca: Usually serves only sandwiches.

Pasticceria: Pastry shop.

Pizza Rustica: Common in central Italy; serves large rectangular pizzas with thicker crusts and more toppings than usually found in a *pizzeria*. You can order as much as you want, and pay by weight.

Pizzeria: We think you can figure this one out.

Ristorante: A restaurant.

Rosticceria: A deli, sometimes with a few tables, where you can order grilled meats (especially chicken).

Tavola Calda: Small restaurant with take-out or fast foods and usually with a few tables.

Trattoria: Less expensive family-run restaurant, usually not too fancy.

Tips for Budget Dining in Italy

There is no need to spend a lot of money in Italy to eat good food. There are all kinds of fabulous foods to be had inexpensively all over Italy.

Eat at a neighborhood restaurant or *trattoria*. You'll always know the price of a meal before entering, as almost all restaurants in Italy post the menu and prices in the window. Never order anything whose price is not known in advance. For instance, if you see *etto* on a menu in Venice this means that you're paying by weight (an *etto* is 100 grams), which can be extremely expensive.

Delis and food stores can provide cheap and wonderful meals. Buy cheese, bread, wine and other snacks and have a picnic. Remember to pack a corkscrew and eating utensils when you leave home.

Lunch, even at the most expensive restaurants listed in this guide, always has a lower price. So, have lunch as your main meal.

Restaurants that have menus written in English (especially those near tourist attractions) are almost always more expensive than neighborhood restaurants.

Street vendors generally sell inexpensive and good food. For the cost of a cup of coffee or a drink, you can linger at a café and watch the world pass you by for as long as you want. It's one of Italy's greatest bargains.

Speaking Italian - Pronunciation Guide

If you're looking for a comprehensive guide to speaking Italian, this is not the the place. These are simply a few tips for speaking Italian followed by a very brief pronunciation guide. It's always good to learn a few polite terms so that you can excuse yourself when you've stepped on the foot of an elderly lady or spilled your drink down the back of the gentleman in front of you. It's also just common courtesy to greet the people you meet in your hotel, and in shops and restaurants, in their own language.

In Italian, you pronounce every letter. E and i are soft vowels when used with consonants. The final e is always pronounced.

The second to the last syllable is stressed. If there is an accent in the word, stress the accented syllable.

a like in father.
au like ow in cow.
b the same as in English.
c **ca, co** and **cu** like k in keep.
– **ce** and **ci**, like ch in cheap.
ch like k in kite.
d the same as in English.
e like in day.
ei like ay in lay.
f the same as in English.
g **ga, go** and **gu** like g in gate.
– **ge** and **gi** like j in jar.
gh like g in goat.
gl like gl in glow except before i, then like lli in million.
gn like ni in onion.
h silent. H after a consonant gives it a hard sound.
i like ee in jeep.
ie, io, iu, i is pronounced as y (ie. *pensione* ~ pen syo neh).
k/l/m/n the same as in English.
o usually like o in boat.
p/q the same as in English.

ue, ui, uo, the u is pronounced like a w (ie. *buono* ~ bwo no).
r with a slight trill.
s like s in sit except between two vowels, then like s in hose.
sc **sca, sco** or **scu** as sk in skirt.
– **sce** or **sci** as sh in sharp.
t the same as English.
u like oo in foot.
v the same as in English.
z the same as ds in fads.

Pronunciation

CA - KA
CE - CHAY
CI - CHEE
CHI - KEY
CHE - KAY

Confused?

11

～ ITALY ～

ABRUZZO & MOLISE
(Off-the-Beaten-Track Italy)

Along the Adriatic coast are
the mountainous regions of
Abruzzo and Molise. The
quiet hill towns are in great
contrast to the Adriatic resorts.
The most notable tourist venue
is the Abruzzo National Park, a
place for hikers and nature lovers.
Outside this nature reserve is Scanno,
a popular summer resort town. L`Aquila
(which means "the eagle") is the capital of Abruzzo and is a business center.
Few tourists from the United States and
Canada visit this part of Italy. If you're
looking for off-the-beaten-track destinations and mountain scenery, Molise and
Abruzzo will certainly please.

Inland, you will find menus dominated
by *capretto* (baby goat), ***agnello arrosto*** (roast lamb), and
porchetta (roast pig). On the coast (in restaurants not serving tourist fare) try *brodetto* (fish soup). *Centerbe* (a green herb liquor)
accompanies many meals. For dessert, try *confetti* (flower-
shaped candy made from sugar-coated almonds).

APULIA (The "Heel" of Italy)

Apulia (Puglia) is the "heel" of Italy. Oppressively hot in July
and August, a rainy day is rare. Apulia is a large wine-producing
region. The area is not frequented by many North American tourists. The baroque town of Martina Franca and the whitewashed
town of Locorotondo are in the wine region and worth a visit. Part
of the coast is heavily industrialized with immense steelworks.

Bari is a modern port and a common departure point for travelers to Greece. *Trulli*, dome-shaped whitewashed stone buildings, are indigienous to the area. The largest collection of *trulli* can be found near Alberobello. The Adriatic fishing ports have architecture similar to the old Venetian ports. Taranto is a modern town, as is the important port of Brindisi, another frequent departure point for visits to Greece. Not to be missed is the lovely Baroque town of Lecce.

Focaccia barese (stuffed pizza), often with *burrata* (very buttery cheese), *triglia* (red mullet), *spigola* (sea bass), *orecchiette con le cime di rapa* (ear-shaped pasta with turnips) and *tiella di riso e cozze* (a mussels, rice and potato dish) can all be found on Apulia's menus. Some avoid the *polpi arricciati* ("curled octopus") when they see that the octopus is beaten and twirled in a basket in order to get the desired "curled" shape. *Bianco di Martina* is a common fortified wine found in Apulia.

BASILICATA
(Undiscovered Italy)

This area was once known as Lucania. One of Italy's smallest regions, Basilicata is also its poorest. Mountainous and barren, Basilicata is not visited by many tourists. The capital city of Potenza was badly damaged in a 1980's earthquake. The hill town of Maratea is dramatically situated on the coast. Here, in small villages such as Metaponto and Matera, you experience the simple Italy.

Spicy *sugna piccante* (pork sauce) flavors many dishes. *Maiale* (pork) is found on most menus, and cured meats like the sausage *luganega*, *luganica* or *lucanica* (there are even more spellings than this!) are common. *Peperoncini* (small hot green peppers preserved in oil) are added to many dishes. Try *scamorza* cheese (the local version of aged *mozzarella*).

CALABRIA (The "Toe" of Italy)

Sun, white-sand beaches, rugged mountains, olive groves and the huge rock of Scilla are all found on the "toe" of Italy. The area was once known as Magna Graecia, and there are villages where a Greek dialect is still spoken. The mountain towns such as Serra San Bruno remain as they were several hundred years ago. Rossano is a beautiful medieval town overlooking a great ravine. Consenza is a town built on a steep hillside with an interesting (almost dilapidated) look to it. Many tourists find themselves in modern Reggio on their way to Sicily. The small towns of Pizzo and Tropea are worth a visit to experience the true Calabria. We would be remiss if we did not mention that some areas of Calabria are strongholds of the local mafia and not recommended for travel.

Costolette d'agnello (lamb chops) and *pesce spada* (swordfish) are found on most menus. *Novellame* is a spread of salted anchovies and *peperoncino* sauce. Pasta is often served with chickpeas (*ceci*). *Stracotto* is a beef stew which in Calabria includes carrots, mushrooms, onions, nutmeg and cloves. *Caviale del sud* or "caviar of the south" is a dish of fried fish preserved in oil and powdered with *peperoncino*. *Fichi* (figs) are featured in many desserts.

CAMPANIA (Naples, Capri & the Amalfi Coast)

Naples, in the shadow of Vesuvius, is congested, noisy, has a reputation as dangerous, and is not an easy city for the tourist. After a quick view of Naples' old town along the harbor, most head for the nearby ruins of Herculaneum and Pompeii. It's an eerie experience walking through nearly perfectly preserved ancient communities buried by the volcanic eruption of Vesuvius. The volcanic island of Ischia and nearby Capri are

often overrun by day trippers in high season. Although it can be expensive, Capri (with its breathtaking vistas) remains the favorite of many returning visitors. The gateway to the Amalfi coast is Sorrento, perched over the sea. The Amalfi coast is the most spectacular coastal drive in Italy (if you have the nerve to drive it in high season). Positano has a great beach with a view of the town perched on the bluff. Amalfi and Ravello, further down the Amalfi coast, have spectacular views. The Amalfi coast reigns as one of the most scenic and photographed coasts in the world.

Seafood is prevalent along the coast, especially *polpi affogati* (octopus in a spicy tomato sauce). Pizza, said to have originated in Naples, is found in many varieties. *Pizza alla Napoletana* is pizza with tomato sauce and anchovies. You will eat tomatoes here like you have never had before. Many pasta dishes are served *al pomodoro* (with a tomato sauce). Meat is often cooked *alla pizzaiola* (in a tomato sauce with garlic). *Partenopea* on a menu simply means served Naples style. For dessert try *sfogliatella* (flaky pastry filled with sweet *ricotta* cheese).

EMILIA-ROMAGNA (From the Adriatic Sea to Central Italy)

The Romans built a grand road from Rimini on the Adriatic Sea to Piacenza in central Italy. The towns that now make up this region developed along this road, the Via Emilia. Piacenza is a major industrial city with a lovely downtown. Parma (which lends its name to the famous Parma ham or *prosciutto*), Modena (home to the Ferrari and Maserati automobiles), Bologna (a learning center, important city for commerce, and *the* food town in Italy), and Ferrara (less spoiled by modern times than the others) are all towns with important historic centers. Imposing Ravenna is in contrast to the most popular Adriatic resort of Rimini. Be careful, as Rimini can be quite dull, even completely closed, off season and extremely overcrowded in season.

The coast features *brodetto* (fish soup). *Prosciutto di Parma* (Parma ham) is common as is *risotto* (the famous Italian rice dish). Suckling pig is called *lattonzolo* here. For dessert, try *castagnole* (chestnut fritters). True Italian food is rare in Rimini, which has revised its menus to cater to the European package tourist.

FRIULI-VENEZIA GIULIA (Trieste & the Austrian Border)

This region borders on Austria and Slovenia. Udine is the capital but Trieste draws the most attention. Trieste, which remained under United Nations control until 1954, is an interesting mix of Austrian and Italian with a Slavic influence from the former Yugoslav republics. The architecture along the port demonstrates the mix of rulers in Trieste. Our several trips to Trieste have made us realize that this area is often, unfortunately, overlooked by tourists. White wine is produced in the hills of Friuli-Venezia Giulia. Visit the towns of Colli Orientali and Collio. The small mountain towns along the Austrian border allow the visitor to experience a mixture of Italy and Austria.

Jota is a minestrone found here and usually contains sauerkraut. *Polenta* (cornmeal mush) is found everywhere. *Brodetto* (fish soup) is common in the coastal area of this region. *Cialzons* is a sweet-and-sour pasta dish found here. The town of San Daniele is the home of *prosciutto di San Daniele* (a cured ham). The Slavic influence is found in the Trieste dessert of *gubana* (sweet bread roll) and the Austrian influence is found in the many coffeehouses of Trieste.

LAZIO (Rome & its Environs)

Lazio (also called Latium) is the region around Rome. To try to list Rome's main attractions would require another guide. Rome can be a frustrating city (it can be hard to carry on a conversation while walking down the street due to the constant traffic noise). But, difficulties aside, few places in the world have so many important sites in such a small area, including the Vatican with its Sistine Chapel, Circus Maximus, the Spanish Steps, the Trevi Fountain, the catacombs...

Sperlonga, San Felice Circeo, Santa Severa and Santa Marinella are all coastal towns worth a visit. Ostia is a large coastal city near Rome and was the main Roman port. Its impressive ruins are an easy day trip from Rome. In inland Lazio, you may visit Tivoli (with Hadrian's Villa), Palestrina, the mountain town of Subiaco and the walled town of Viterbo.

Rome is said to have 5,000 restaurants where you can eat just about anything. After a grueling day of sightseeing, stop in a small restaurant (*trattoria*), drink some wine and eat a hearty dish of pasta such as one served ***all' arrabbiata*** (in a spicy tomato and herb sauce) or ***alla carbonara*** (with bacon, cheese, olive oil and eggs). Meals often start with ***bruschetta*** (garlic toast) and end with *grappa* (of which we drank a little too much on our first night here). When in Rome...

LE MARCHE (The Apennines Mountain Region)

The Apennines Mountains separate Le Marche from the rest of Central Italy. Ancona, on the Adriatic coast (a common departure point for Venice) is a modern port town. Pilgrims visit the house of the Virgin Mary in Loreto (brought here, according to legend, by angels). Urbino, one of the lesser-known great Renaissance cities, looks much as it did in the fifteenth century. In the Tronto River Valley, scenic Ascoli Piceno is another Le Marche town worth visiting. Most travelers head for the crowded (package tour-filled) coastal towns. These crowded resorts are in great contrast to the sedate hill towns.

Truffles (*tartufi*) are a specialty here, and summer peaches (*pesche*) and plums (*susine*) are some of the best fruits you will ever taste. *Vincigrassi* (baked lasagna dish), *olive all'ascolana* (large stuffed olives), *porchetta* (roast suckling pig) and rabbit (*coniglio)* are popular. *Brodetto di pesce* (fish soup) is found along the coast. In Ancona, *brodetto* contains thirteen varieties of fish.

LIGURIA (The Italian Riviera)

Wedged between mountains and the sea, the coastal region of Liguria stretches from the French border to Tuscany and is a popular tourist destination. Genoa, a large industrial city, is also Italy's biggest port. Tourists usually visit only the old, central part of the city. West of Genoa toward the French border are the bright tourist towns of Ventimiglia and Bordighera. San Remo (with its famous casino) is the largest resort. East from Genoa, you will find the resort of Nervi with beautiful parks. Further down the coast are the resort towns of Camogli, Rapallo, Santa Margherita and of course, perhaps the best known and most beautiful Italian port of Portofino. One drawback is the gridlock in and out of Portofino in high season. Sestri Levante makes a good base for exploring the highlight of any trip to Liguria, the Cinque Terre, five beautiful towns, which until recently were accessible only by train or a series of hiking paths. Perched on dramatic cliffs above the sea, you will experience car-free serenity and an Italy of old. Down the coast is Lerici (where we had one of our most memorable meals in an open-air restaurant on the port).

Seafood is dominant in Liguria, especially *branzino* (sea bass), *aragosta* (lobster), *vongole* (clams), *zuppa di datteri* (fish soup), *stoccafisso* (dried cod), *ciuppin* (fish and vegetable stew) and *fritto misto di frutti di mare* (mixed seafood, usually grilled).

Sadly, seafood is becoming less common because of pollution and overfishing in the Mediterranean. *Basilico* (basil) grown in the hills above the sea forms the basis of *pesto* and is common in the cuisine of Liguria. Try *ravioli di magro* (pasta stuffed with herbs and *ricotta* cheese).

LOMBARDY (Milan & the Lake District)

Fashionable, modern Milan is an important center of Italian commerce. If you like to shop, Milan is the place. Tourists often visit four important sites: the Duomo (cathedral, especially the ornate roof), La Scala (the opera house), the Last Supper (at the church of Santa Maria delle Grazie), and the Galleria Vittorio Emanuele (the famous glass-domed shopping center).

In great contrast to Milan is the Lake District, including Lakes Orta (often, regrettably, ignored), Maggiore, Como, and  Garda. The towns that line these lakes remain dotted with former palaces (many now resorts) with impressive formal gardens. Many believe the Lake District is Italy at its best. On Lake Como, Bellagio is the most famous resort, but Varenna, with its tiny harbor and splendid beach, is the favorite of many.

Trota (trout) is popular in the Lake District. Lombardy specialties include *stracotto* (pot roast), *ossobuco* (braised veal shank) and *capretto* (roast kid). You will find many dishes served *alla milanese* (battered with eggs and breadcrumbs and fried). *Risotto alla milanese* is a popular rice dish made golden from the ingredient saffron. *Gorgonzola* (a delicious blue cheese) is often found in pasta dishes. Lombardy cheeses also included *crescenza* (a soft, buttery cheese) and *mascarpone* (a very creamy cheese). *Torrone* (honey-and-almond nougat) is a common dessert.

PIEDMONT & VALLE D'AOSTA (Turin & the Alps)

Sometimes the Alpine regions of Piedmont (which means "foot of the mountain") and Valle d'Aosta (north of Piedmont) feel more like France or Switzerland than Italy. Valle d'Aosta has two official languages: Italian and French. Many come to the largest city in these regions, Turin (Torino), to see the Shroud of Turin (believed by some to be the cloth in which Christ's body was wrapped after the crucifixion). North of Turin, into Valle d'Aosta, is Saint Vincent (a popular gambling resort). Any trip to this area would not be complete without a visit to Breuil-Cervina at the base of the Matterhorn (Monte Cervino) with breathtaking views of this famous mountain peak. Courmayeur, another Alpine resort, is the gateway to Mont Blanc (Monte Bianco) on the French border. The walled city of Aosta is nestled in the Alps. Asti (yes, as in the wine), Novara, Vercelli, and Casale Monferrato are all towns with impressive medieval towers. If you're looking for beautiful mountain scenery, don't miss these regions.

Piemontese on a menu means "Piedmont style" or with white truffles. *Tartufi bianchi* are famous white truffles from Alba and Asti. *Alla Valdostana* on a menu means "Valle d'Aosta style" and usually means with ham and cheese. Roast game, sausages and butter play heavy roles in the local diet. *Tajarin* is thin ribbon pasta made golden with egg yolks. *Fonduta* (fondue) is popular. The French influence can be found in *crespelle* (crêpes). You will find *cervo* (venison), *carbonade* (beef cooked in wine and onions) and *arrosto misto* (grilled meats) here along with *trota* (trout). *Gianduiotti* are hazelnut chocolates found in Turin and one of our favorite treats. *Torta di nocciole*, hazelnut cake, is a must.

SAN MARINO (Europe's Oldest Country)

With about only 25,000 people and 24 square miles, San Marino (totally surrounded by Italy) claims to be Europe's oldest existing country. San Marino's official name is the Most Serene Republic of San Marino, and is located 15 miles inland from the Adriatic Sea resort of Rimini. Its chief industries are tourism and the sale of postage stamps. Mt. Titano, upon which San Marino sits, must be climbed after you leave your car. There are three medieval fortresses on the mountain. The capital, also named San Marino, is a maze of attractive narrow streets.

Food is typical Italian. You'll find *coniglio* (rabbit) and *nidi di rondine* (pasta rolls). Don't miss *caciatella* (San Marino's version of crème caramel).

SARDINIA (SARDEGNA)

The island of Sardinia is located about 115 miles off the western coast of Italy in the Mediterranean. Ten miles to the north is the French island of Corsica. Sardinia has been a part of Italy since 1861. Cagliari, the capital, is on the south coast, which is known for its ancient ruins. For the most part, Sardinia remains unspoiled from its rocky coast to its mountainous interior. The northeastern Costa Smeralda (Emerald Coast) is the only area where tourist development has arrived. Those looking for peace and quiet and even isolation should experience the mountainous inland region of Barbagia.

Lobster (*aragosta*) is plentiful along the coast, and the northern coast of Sardinia is sometimes referred to as the lobster coast. Lamb (*agnello*), rabbit (*cunillu*) and trout (*trota*) are ubiquitous. Grilled meats are a specialty. The shepherds of Sardinia feast on *pane carasau*, which is also known as *carta da musica* (music paper). Durham wheat, salt, water and yeast are the simple ingredients for this wood fire-baked bread. You will find this thin, crispy bread used as a pizza crust.

Other specialties of Sardinia include *porceddu* (roast suckling pig which is the "national" dish of Sardinia), *cascà* (couscous), and many honey-based desserts such as *sebadas* (deep-fried cheese-filled ravioli soaked in honey).

SICILY (SICILIA)

F rench, Arabs, Spanish and Italians have all controlled Sicily, the largest and most populated island in the Mediterranean. Travelers will find some of the best-preserved Greek and Roman ruins here, along with the ornate architecture of its churches and palaces. Agrigento is home to the most important archaeological site in Sicily, the Greek "Valley of the Temples." Siracusa (Syracuse) is also known for its Greek and Roman ruins. The capital is Palermo, but most travelers head to the medieval town of Taormina on the east coast in the shadows of Mount Etna, an active volcano. Messina (destroyed by both an earthquake and the bombs of World War II) has bland, modern architecture, and is in strong contrast to the picturesque fishing port of Cefalù.

Sicilian cuisine is not simply pasta and olive oil but incorporates Italian, Greek, French, Spanish and Arab influences. Some specialties are *pasta con le sarde* (pasta with fresh sardines), *pesce spada* (swordfish), and the simple *cicina* (a mixture of fried small fish). Other specialties are *capo-nata* (sweet-and-sour sauce with eggplant, tomatoes, onions and peppers), *pasta alla Norma* (pasta with a tomato, basil and eggplant sauce topped with *ricotta* cheese) and *costoletta alla siciliana* (thin slices of veal or beef topped with chopped garlic and *parmesan* cheese, then breaded and deep-fried).

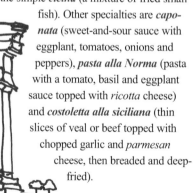

Desserts, and Sicilians

are famous for their desserts, include *cannoli* (pastry tubes filled
with sweetened *ricotta* cheese) and *cassata alla siciliana* (layered
spongecake).

Marsala wine (from the town of the same name) is a fortified
wine that can range from rich and sweet to dry.

TICINO (Italian-Speaking Switzerland)

Ticino is the main Italian-speaking canton or region of
Switzerland. Palm trees, Italian architecture, Swiss orderli-
ness and Italian food all make Ticino (with its famous resorts
of Lugano and Locarno) a great travel destination. Ticino is
Switzerland's southernmost canton, bordering on Italy, and has
been a part of Switzerland since the early 1800s. This region has
always remained strongly Italian. Italian is one of four
official languages of Switzerland (along with French, German and
Romansh).

Specialties found in Ticino are *risotto ai fiori di zucca* (a rice dish
made with a heavy cream base and zucchini flowers stirred in
along with *parmesan* cheese), *pancetta arrotolata* (rolled bacon
flavored with cloves), *capretto* (baby goat), *fritto misto* (breaded
and fried lake fish), *cotto antico* (bay leaf-flavored salami), and
giambonetti di pollo (stuffed chicken leg). Bread is a staple in all
meals, especially bread with a thick crust dusted with flour called
crusca. Two common cheeses found in Ticino are *formaggini di
capra* (fresh goat's-milk cheese) and *formaggini d'Alpe* (a common
cow's-milk cheese). Both of these cheeses are eaten with olive oil,
salt and pepper.

TRENTINO-ALTO ADIGE (The Dolomites)

The Alto Adige is the far north of Italy and is more like Austria
than Italy. The Dolomite Mountains dominate this area. At
the Brenner Pass, on the border with Austria, is the town of
Bolzano/Bozen (Austrian until 1918). Near Bolzano is the

wine town of Caldaro. Bressanone/Brixen is a beautiful mountain town and the Alto Adige's oldest city. Ortisei, San Martino and Madonna di Campiglio are all summer and winter resort towns. Breathtaking views abound in Brunico/Bruneck. Merano has an interesting old town and famous spas. Trento, the capital of Trentino, is more Italian than Austrian and remains an attractive and architecturally interesting town.

Food here is more German than Italian (especially the farther north you travel). Game, dumplings (*knoedel*) and cured ham (*speck*) all stress the German influence. Sauerkraut (*crauti*) is featured heavily in dishes, as are *wurstel* (hot dogs and brats). For dessert, apples, grown in large numbers in the region, are often added to the Germanic dessert of *strudel*.

TUSCANY (One of the World's Most Popular Destinations)

There are so many picturesque towns in Tuscany, space allows only a few highlights. With unspoiled hills, perfectly preserved towns and great food and wine, Tuscany is one of the most popular tourist destinations in Italy and the world. Since childhood, we wanted to see the Leaning Tower of Pisa (and the nearby and lesser-known baptistery). There's so much more to this vibrant and interesting city than just the tower. Siena's main square, the Piazza del Campo, and ornate cathedral are only two gems in the beautiful town with (thankfully) a car-free center. San Gimignano, with its walls and towers, is an incredibly picturesque town. The hilltop towns of Lucca, Montepulciano, Montalcino and Pienza are all worth a visit. Of course, Florence is the favorite of many visitors to Italy. Its wealth of art, housed in buildings which themselves are art, leaves many visitors wanting to return again and again.

Start your meal with *crostini* (toasted bread with various toppings). *La bistecca alla Fiorentina*, a T-bone steak, must not be missed, nor should any of the *pecorino* cheeses. Menus often include dishes served *alla lepre* (in a rabbit-based sauce), *cinghiale* (wild boar), *arista* (roast, seasoned pork loin), and *ribollita* (bean and/or cabbage soup which means "twice-cooked soup). *Chianti*, *chianti* and more *chianti*. Enough said!

UMBRIA (Assisi & the Hill Towns North of Rome)

Green hills, towns spared from industrialization, and wonderful dining combine to make Umbria an outstanding Italian destination (especially by car). Perugia is Umbria's largest city with a historic city center, but most tourists come here to visit the smaller towns like Gubbio in northern Umbria. Orvieto is located on a monumental square-shaped rock visible for miles. Don't miss this impressive and well-preserved town (or a taste of its famous wines). Assisi is home to a huge basilica built in memory of local hero St. Francis. It's ironic that such a huge basilica was built for such a humble man, or that the streets are filled with shops selling St. Francis keychains. Still, Assisi, perched on a hill, is a memorable sight. Walled Spoleto (home of the well-known art festival) is dominated by a large castle and is surrounded by wooded countryside.

Tartufi (truffles) are a specialty here, especially the black truffle (*tartufo nero*). *Stringozzi* (homemade pasta) is used in many dishes, especially in Spoleto. *Strozzapreti* (dumplings with meat sauce) is a dish with the strange name of "priest stranglers" after a priest allegedly choked on it. *Palombacci* are small songbirds cooked whole on a spit. For dessert, try *stinchetti* (marzipan cakes). Of course, no one thinks of eating in Umbria without drinking one of the many fine wines of this region.

VENETO (Venice & its Environs)

Veneto is the region around Venice. Despite the tourists, the sometimes smelly canals and the often

inflated prices, Venice is unlike anywhere else in the world. Many cities claim to be pedestrian only, but Venice is truly car-free. Don't just take a day trip here. Once the day trippers leave, Venice becomes a quiet, romantic maze of streets with spectacular architecture. As many times as we have visited, we are always amazed at the splendid beauty of Venice with its buildings rising out of the sea. Don't miss the Piazza San Marco, the Bridge of Sighs, the Basilica di San Marco and the Doge's Palace. If time permits, visit the islands of Murano (famous for its ornate glass), Burano (famous for its lace), San Michele (Venice's island cemetery) and Torcello (for a taste of an almost deserted island).

Veneto includes the cities of Vicenza, Padua (where you can see the "uncorrupted" tongue of St. Anthony), Verona and Treviso. Many towns remain unspoiled and rarely visited by tourists, including Valpolicella (home of this popular Italian red wine), the hills of Colli Euganei (home of hot thermal springs), and Asolo. North of Treviso are the mountain resorts of Cortina d'Ampezzo and Belluno.

Cape sante (scallops), *baccalà* (dried cod), *fegato alla veneziana* (liver with onions), *seppie* (cuttlefish), and *granseola* (crab) are all specialties of Venice. *Polenta* (the famous cornmeal mush) is found throughout the region. *Carpaccio* is thinly sliced raw beef served in a sauce, and was named by the owner of Harry's Bar in Venice after a famous Venetian painter. *Prosecco* is a slightly sparkling wine from Veneto and worth a try. While in Venice, don't miss having an evening drink or *caffè* in the Piazza San Marco.

This is a brief listing of some familiar English food and food-related words that you may need in a restaurant, followed by a list of phrases that may come in handy.

anchovy, acciuga (acciughe)
appetizer, antipasto (i)
apple, mela (e)
artichoke, carciofo (i)
ashtray, portacenere
asparagus, asparago (i)
bacon, pancetta
baked, al forno
banana, banana (e)
bean, fagiolo (i)
beef, manzo (di bue)
beefsteak, bistecca (di manzo)
beer, birra (e)
beverage, bevanda (e)
bill, conto (i)
bitter, amaro (a)
boiled, bollito/lesso
bottle, bottiglia
bowl, scodella
bread, pane
bread rolls, panino (i)
breakfast, prima colazione
broiled, graticola/griglia
broth, brodo
butter, burro
cabbage, cavolo (i)
cake, torta (e)
candle, candela
carrot, carota (e)
cereal, cereale (i)
chair, sedia

[handwritten notes:]
Words that end in A or O are singular

Words that end in E or I are plural

bottiglia ~ bow·tee·Lee-ah

Words and letters in parentheses indicate plurals.

cereale ~ cheer·ee·ah·Lay

27

check, conto (i)

cheers, salute/cin cin

cheese, formaggio (formaggi)

cherry, ciliegia (e)

chicken soup, brodo di pollo/zuppa di pollo

chicken, pollo

chop, costoletta (e)

clam, vongola (e)

cocktail, cocktail

cod, baccalà/merluzzo

coffee, caffè (also black coffee)

coffee w/hot water
  (to dilute), caffè amercano

coffee w/milk, caffè latte

coffee (decaf), caffè hag/caffè decaffeinato

coffee w/cream, caffè con panna

cold, freddo (a)

corn, mais

cover charge, pane coperto

cucumber, cetriolo (i)

cup, coppa
  tazza coffee/tea cup

custard, crema

dessert, dolce (i)

dinner, cena

dish (plate), piatto

drink, bevanda (e)

dry (as in wine), secco

duck, anitra/anatra

egg, uovo (a)

espresso, caffè espresso

fish, pesce

fish soup, zuppa di pesce

fork, forchetta

french fries, patate fritte

fresh, fresco (a)

fried, fritto (a)/fritti (e)

caffè italiano.   *caffè americano.*

freddo ~
FRAY-doh

dolce ~
dole-chay

cena ~
chain-ah

forchetta.

forchetta ~
FOR-KAY-TAH

fruit, frutta
game, cacciagione/selvaggina
garlic, aglio
gin, gin
glass, bicchiere
grapefruit, pompelmo
grape, uva
green bean, fagiolino (i)
grilled, griglia or alla griglia
half, mezzo (a)
ham (cooked), prosciutto cotto
ham (cured), prosciutto crudo
hamburger, hamburger
honey, miele
hors d'oeuvre, antipasto
hot, caldo (a)
iced, ghiacciato
ice coffee, caffè freddo
ice cream, gelato (i)
ice (on the rocks), ghiaccio or con ghiaccio
ice water, acqua fredda
iced tea, tè freddo
ketchup, ketchup/salsa di pomodoro
knife, coltello
lamb, abbacchio/agnello
large, grande
lemon, limone (i)
lettuce, lattuga
little (a little), un pó
liver, fegato (fegatini)
lobster, aragosta (e)
loin, lombata
lunch, pranzo
marinated, marinato (a)
match, fiammifero (i)
meat, carne
medium (cooked), a puntino or normale

Bicchiere.
BEE·KEE·AY·RAY

griglia
GREE-LEE·AH

ghiacciato ~
ghee-AH-chee-A·Tol

coltello.

melon, melone

menu, carta or menù

milk, latte

mineral water, acqua minerale

mineral water (sparkling), acqua minerale gasata

mineral water (w/out carbonation), acqua minerale non gasata

mixed, mista (o)

mushroom, fungo (i)

mussel, cozza (e)

mustard, senape

napkin, tovagliolo

noodles, taglierini/pasta

octopus, polipo/polpo

oil, olio

olive oil, olio d'oliva

omelette, frittata

on the rocks (w/ ice), con ghiaccio

onion, cipolla (e)

orange, arancia (arance)

orange juice, succo d'arancia

overdone, ben cotto

oyster, ostrica (ostriche)

pastries, dolci/paste

peach, pesca (pesche)

pear, pera (e)

pea, pisello (i)

pepper (black), pepe

pepper (bell), peperone (i)

perch, pesce persico

pineapple, ananas

plate (dish), piatto

please, per piacere

plum, susina (e)

poached, affogato

pork, maiale

funghi.

Tovagliolo ~
Toe·vah·Lee·oh·Lo

Cipolla ~
chee·polla

per piacere ~
pare·pee·ah·chair·AY

maiale ~
my·AL·LAY

potato, patata (e)
poultry, pollame
prawn, gamberetto (i)
rabbit, coniglio
rare, al sangue
raspberry, lampone (i)
receipt, ricevuta/scontrino
rice, riso
roast, arrosto
salad, insalata
salt, sale
sandwich, sandwich/panino (i)
sauce, salsa
saucer, piattino/sottocoppa
sautéed, saltato (i)/saltata (e)
scallops, cappe sante
scrambled, strapazzate
seafood, frutti di mare
seasoning, condimento (i)
shrimp, scampo (i),
   gamberetto (i)
small, piccolo (i)/piccola (e)
smoked, affumicata (o)
snail, lumaca (lumache)
sole, sogliola (e)
soup, zuppa (e)/minestra (e)
spaghetti, spaghetti
sparkling wine, spumante
specialty, specialità
spinach, spinaci
spoon, cucchiaio
squid, calamaro (i)
steak, bistecca
steamed, a vapore
stewed, in umido
strawberry, fragola (e)
sugar, zucchero

Coniglio.
Co-NEE-LEO

ricevuta ~
ree-chay-voo-tah

gamberetto.

Lumaca.

Cucchiaio ~
KOO KEE AYE OH

Zucchero ~
ZOO-KARE-OH

sugar substitute, dolcificante

supper, cena

sweet, dolce

table, tavolo

tea, tè

tea w/lemon, tè al limone

tea w/milk, tè al latte

teaspoon, cucchiaino

thank you, grazie

tip, mancia

toasted, tostato

tomato, pomodoro (i)

trout, trota

tumbler (glass), bicchiere

tuna, tonno

turkey, tacchino

utensil, posata (e)/utensile (i)

veal, vitello

veal scallop, scaloppa di vitello

vegetable, legume (i). *Verdura (e)* green vegetables

vegetarian, vegetariana (o)

venison, carne di cervo

vinegar, aceto

waiter, cameriere

waitress, cameriera

water, acqua

well done, ben cotto

whipped cream, panna montata

wine, vino

wine (full-bodied), vino corposo

wine list, lista dei vini

wine (red), vino rosso

wine (rosé), vino rosé

wine (white), vino bianco

dolce – DOL-CHAY

TAZZA
di t̀.

tacchino
TA-KEE·NO

Unless there's a written translation, it pretty much sounds like it looks, only more Italian sounding. Don't forget to pronounce that final 'E'!

Helpful Phrases

Prego (*preh-go*) can mean: thank you, you're welcome, this way (with a hand gesture), please, okay, and can I help you.
Ciao means hello *and* goodbye. *chow*
Italians answer the phone with *Pronto?* *prohn-toh*

please, per favore *pehr-fah-voh-ray*

thank you, grazie *graht-see-ay*

yes, sì *see*

no, no *noh*

good morning, buon giorno *bwohn-jor-noh*

good afternoon/evening, buona sera *bwohn-ah- say-rah*

good night, buona notte *bwohn-ah noht-tay*

goodbye, arrivederci *ah-ree-veh-dehr-chee*

do you speak English?, parla inglese? *par-lah een-gleh-zay*

I don't speak Italian, non parlo l'italiano *nohn par-loh lee-tah-lee-ah-noh*

excuse me, mi scusi (or *scusi*) *mee-skoo-zee*

I don't understand, non capisco *nohn kah-pees-koh*

waiter, cameriere *kah-meh-ree-eh-ray*

waitress, cameriera *kah-meh-ree-eh-rah*

I'd like..., Vorrei... *voh-reh-ee*

I'd like a table, Vorrei un tavolo *voh-reh-ee oon-tah-voh-loh*

I'd like to make a reservation, Vorrei prenotare *voh-reh-ee preh-noh-tah-ray*

for one person, per uno (una)   *OONO*
                                      DOO AY
for two, per due (2), tre (3), quattro (4), cinque (5),   *TRAY*
                                      KWATRO
sei (6), sette (7), otto (8), nove (9), dieci (10)   *CHINK·WAY*
                                      SAY
today/tomorrow, oggi *oh-jee*/domani *doh-mah-nee*   *SET·TAY*
                                      OH TOE
by the window, vicino alla finestra *vee-chee-noh*   *NO VAY*
ah-lah fee-neh-strah   *dee AY CHI*

outside, fuori *fwoh-ree*/**inside,** dentro *dehn-troh*

where is?, dov'è *doh-vey*

the bathroom, il bagno/la toilette *eel bahn-nyoh/lah twah-leh-tay*

the bill, il conto *eel kohn-toh*

service (not) included, servizio (non) incluso *sehr-veet-see-oh (nohn) een-kloo-zoh*

33

a mistake, errore *eh-roh-ray*

credit card, carta di credito *kar-tah dee kreh-dee-toh*

how much does this cost?, quanto costa? *kwahn-toh koh-stah*

what is this?, cos' è questo? *koh-zeh kweh-stoh*

I did not order this, Io questo non l'ho ordinato *ee-oh kweh-stoh nohn loh or-dee-nah-toh*

this is, questo è *kweh-stoh eh*

a little, un po' *oon poh*

hot, caldo (a) *kahl-do*/**cold,** freddo (a) *freh-doh*

spicy (hot), piccante *pee-kahn-tay*

vegetarian, vegetariano/a *soh-noh veh-jeh-tah-ryah-noh/ah*

I don't eat,... Non mangio *nohn mahn-joh*

allergic, allergico (a) *ah-lehr-jee-koh*

dairy, latticini *lah-tee-chee-nee*

wheat/gluten, frumento *froo-mehn-toh*/glutine *gloo-tee-nay*

seafood, frutti di mare *froo-tee dee mah-ray*

shellfish, molluschi e crostacei *moh-loo-skee ay kroh-stah-cheh-ee*

nuts, noci e altra frutta secca *noh-chee ay ahl-trah froo-tah seh-kah*

peanuts, arachidi *ah-rah-kee-dee*

diabetic, diabete *dee-ah-beh-tay*

kosher, kasher *kah-shehr*

no caffeine, senza caffeina *sehnt-sah kah-feh-ee-nah*

no alcohol, niente alcool *nee-ehn-tay ahl-kohl*

vegetarian, vegetariano (a) *veh-jeh-tah-ree-ah-noh*

vegan, vegano (a) *veh-gah-noh*

undercooked, troppo crudo *troh-poh kroo-doh*

overcooked, troppo cotto *troh-poh koh-toh*

delicious, delizioso (a) *deh-leet-see-oh-zoh*

light (low-fat), leggero *leh-jeh-roh*

open, aperto *ah-pehr-toh*/**closed,** chiuso *kee-oo-zoh*

Monday, lunedì *loo-nay-dee*

Tuesday, martedì *mart-ay-dee*

Wednesday, mercoledì *mehr-cohl-ay-dee*

Thursday, giovedì *joh-vay-dee*

Friday, venerdì *ven-nehr-dee*

Saturday, sabato *sah-bah-toh*

Sunday, domenica *doh-mehn-nee-kah*

abbacchio, lamb

abbacchio alla cacciatora, pieces of lamb braised w/rosemary, garlic, wine & peppers

abbacchio alla romana, pieces of lamb cooked until brown, then roasted in a rosemary, garlic, vinegar & anchovy sauce

abbacchio brodettato, pieces of lamb cooked in a broth of lemon, parsley & beaten eggs

abboccato, a medium-sweet wine

abbrustolito, toasted

abruzzese, red pepper sauce

acciuga (acciughe), anchovy

acciuga ~
AH·CHEE·oo·ga

acciughe al limone, anchovies w/lemon-based sauce

acerbo, sour

aceto, vinegar

aceto balsamico, balsamic vinegar. Aged vinegar used in many dishes, especially salads

acetosella, sorrel

acido, sour

acini di pepe, pasta for soup in the shape of peppercorns

acqua, water

acqua brillante, tonic water

acquacotta, bread & vegetable soup

acquadella, small whitebait fish

acqua di rubinetto, tap water

acqua di seltz, seltzer water/soda water

"Acqua cotta"
means
cooked water

acqua fredda, ice water

acqua gasata, carbonated water

acqua ghiacciata, ice water

acqua minerale, mineral water

acqua minerale frizzante, extremely carbonated water

acqua minerale naturale, mineral water w/out carbonation

acqua naturale, tap water

acqua non gasata, water w/out carbonation

acqua non potabile, do not drink the water!

acqua pazza, sauce of tomato, garlic, oil, parsley & chili pepper

acqua semplice, tap water

acqua tonica, tonic water

Acquavite, brandy/distilled spirit flavored w/caraway

affettato, sliced

affettato (i), cold cut

affogato, poached. This can also refer to ice cream soaked in coffee or liqueur

affumicato, smoked

agliata/all'aglio, garlic sauce

aglio, garlic

aglio e olio, w/garlic & olive oil

aglione, mixture of garlic, sea salt, rosemary & sage

agnello, lamb

Aglio.

agnello alla turca, lamb stew w/raisins

agnello con salsa di uovo, lamb w/egg sauce.

agnolotti, filled pasta (square shaped)

agone, freshwater fish found in the lake country (the size of sardines)

agresto, juice of unripened grapes

agro, lemon juice & olive oil dressing

agrodolce, sweet & sour sauce

ai/al/all'/alla, in the style of/with

ajula, sea bream

ala, wing

alaccia, large sardine

alalunga, albacore (a type of tuna)

Agresto is sometimes used in place of vinegar

Albana, dry to semi-sweet wine from Emilia-Romagna

albicocca (albicocche), apricot

albume, egg white

alcolica, alcoholic. *Una bevanda alcolica* is an alcoholic beverage

alcool, alcol

Aleatico, dessert wine (made from muscat grapes)

alette, wing

alfabetini, alphabet noodles for soup

al forno, baked

alfredo, w/butter & cream sauce

al fresco, outside (in the fresh air)

alice (i), anchovy

allodola (e), lark

alloro, bay leaf

amabile, slightly sweet wine

amarena (e), sour cherry

amaretti, macaroons

ALLORO.

amaretto, sweet almond-flavored liqueur

amaro, bitter/bitter cordial (bitters)

amatriciana, bacon, tomato & spices sauce

amburghese/amburgo, hamburger/ground meat
amburghese alla tirolese, hamburger served w/onion rings
Americano, Campari, vermouth & lemon peel
ammiru, prawns in Sicily
analcolico (i), non-alcoholic
ananas, pineapple
anatra, duck
anatroccolo, duckling
anelli/anellini, small circular
    pasta for soup (ring pasta)
aneto, dill
anguidda, another name for eel in Sicily
anguilla (e), eel
anguilla alla veneziana, eel braised
    w/tuna & lemon sauce
anguria, watermelon
anice, anise
animelle, sweetbreads
animelle alla salvia, sweetbreads w/sage
anisetta, anise-flavored liquor
anitra, duck
anitra germano, mallard duck
anitra selvatica, wild duck
annegati, slices of meat in wine
antipasto (i), appetizer
antipasto alla marinara/antipasto di mare/antipasto di
    pesce, assorted seafood
antipasto misto, assorted appetizers
aperitivo, aperitif
arachide (i), peanut
aragosta (e), lobster (crayfish)
arancia (e), orange. *All' arancia* means w/orange juice
aranciata, orangeade/orange soda
arancino (i) di riso, breaded ball of cooked rice stuffed w/meat
& deep-fried. It gets its name from its resemblance to an
orange
argentina, argentine fish
arigusta, crawfish
aringa, herring
aringa affumicata, smoked herring
arista, roast, seasoned pork loin
arista alla fiorentina, roasted pork rubbed w/garlic paste,
    cloves, salt, rosemary, pepper

In Perugia Anguilla can also refer to an eel shaped pastry created originally by nuns.

arista di maiale/arista di suino, pork loin

arrabbiata, all', w/a spicy tomato & herb sauce

arrostetti, small roast

arrosti misti freddi, a selection of cold roasted meats

arrostini, veal chops

arrostino, small roast

arrostino annegato, small veal roast
served with mushrooms

arrostite, grilled/roasted

arrosto/arrostito, roast/roasted

arrosto alla genovese, a roast w/onions, mushrooms
& tomatoes

arrosto alla montanara, pot roast

arrosto con pastine, roast w/dough crust

arrosto di manzo, roast beef

arrosto in porchetta, roast suckling pig stuffed w/garlic,
bacon & herbs

arrosto misto, mixed roast meats

arrosto morto, pot roast

arsella (e), mussel

asciutta (o), dry. Also refers to pasta w/sauce
(as opposed to pasta for soup)

asiago, sharp cheese (round-shaped cheese)

asiago dolce, mild *asiago*

asparago (i), asparagus

asparago alla bismark, asparagus w/melted butter & fried egg

asparago alla milanese/asparago all'uovo, asapagus topped
w/melted butter, *parmesan* cheese & fried egg

assortito (i), assorted

astaco/astice, lobster

Asti Spumante, sparkling white wine

attorta, fruit- & almond-filled pastry

Aurum, orange liqueur

avvoltino, standing roast or rolled roast

babà, spongecake covered w/rum

babaluci, snails in tomato & onion sauce

bacca (e), berry

baccalà, salt cod

ASTI.

baccalà alla fiorentina, salt cod floured & fried in oil
& tomato sauce

baccalà alla lucana, salt cod cooked w/peppers

baccalà alla vicentina, salt cod w/onion, parsley, garlic,
anchovies & cinnamon

bacio, chocolate hazelnut (means "kiss")
bagna cauda/bagna caoda, hot vegetable dip w/anchovies
bagnet, sauce (in Piedmont)
balsamella, bechamel/white sauce
banana (e), banana   *Good Guess!*
bar, serves espresso, cappuccino, rolls, small sandwiches,
    alcoholic beverages and soft drinks
barbabietola (e), beet
Barbaresco, soft red wine from Piedmont
    (lighter & drier than *Barolo*)
Barbera, dry red wine   *Andy hates*
barbe rosse, beets   *beets even*
Bardolino, pale, light red wine   *in Italy.*
Barolo, rich red wine from Piedmont
basilico, basil
bastoncini, bread sticks (means "little sticks")
battuta scanello, pounded round steak
battutina al prosciutto, hamburger mixed w/cured ham
battuto, finely chopped herbs, onions, celery & carrots
battuto di manzo, ground beef
bavette (i), thin, flat pasta
beccaccia, woodcock
beccaccino, snipe (game)
beccafico, warbler/song bird
belga, Belgian endive   *"Bel Paese"*
bellini, *Prosecco* & peach juice.
    Try one at Harry's Bar in Venice   *means*
bel paese, smooth, mild & soft cheese   *beautiful*
ben cotto, well done   *country*
bensone, lemon cake
besciamella, white cream sauce
bevanda (e), drink/beverage
bevanda compresa, cost of drinks included
bianchetti, small anchovy (or sardine)
bianchi, white
bianco, white wine
Bianco di Martina, a fortified wine found in Apulia
bianco, in, w/butter (w/out a sauce)
bibita (e), drink/beverage
bibite analcoliche, soft drinks
bicchiere, glass   *Bicchiere.*
biete, Swiss chard   *BEE·KEE·AY·RAY*
bietole, beet/Swiss chard

bietole alla padella, Swiss chard cooked w/butter &/or oil
bietoline, beet greens
bietolini, Swiss chard
bignè/bignole (con crema), cream puff
bigoli, larger form of spaghetti
biova/biovetta, round bread loaf
birra, beer
birra alla spina, tap beer
birra analcolica, no-alcohol beer
birra bionda, light beer
birra chiara, light beer (lager)
birra di barile, draft beer
birra importata, imported beer
birra in bottiglia, bottled beer
birra in lattina, beer in a can
birra scura, dark beer
biscotto (i), cookie/biscuit/cracker/spongecake
biscotti di prato, cookies w/pieces of almond
biscuit tortoni, dessert of beaten egg whites & macaroon
    crumbs topped w/whipped cream & toasted almonds
bismark, alla, usually means served w/a fried egg
bistecca, steak
bistecca alla bismark, fried steak w/an egg on top
bistecca alla fiorentina, T-bone steak
bistecca alla pizzaiola, steak w/tomato & garlic sauce
bistecca di manzo, beef steak
bistecca di vitello, veal scallop
bistecca Fiorentina, T-bone steak
bistecca impanata, cutlet/chop
bistecche, steaks
bistecchine, thin steaks
bitto, firm, smoked cheese
bobe, sea bream
boccolotti, short tubular pasta
bocconcini, diced veal w/tomato
    & white wine sauce/*mozzarella* balls
boldro, monkfish in Tuscany
boletus, porcini mushrooms
bollito (i), boiled. Can also mean meat or fish stew
bollito di gallina, boiled chicken
bollito di manzo, boiled beef
bollito misto, mixed boiled meats
bolognese, alla, usually means a tomato & meat sauce

BiRRA

Bistecca Impanata is often breaded and fried in butter

"bocconcini" means mouthful

bomba di riso, rice dish w/ground meat & herb fillings

bombette, pork shoulder stuffed with melted cheese.
A specialty in Apulia

bombolone (i), doughnut

bonèt, chocolate cream dessert. A specialty in Piedmont

borlotti, type of bean

boscaiola, means "woodsman style" & can refer to many
things, including w/wild mushrooms

bosega, mullet

botolo, mullet

bottarga, fish eggs (tuna roe that has been salted & pressed)

bottiglia, bottle

bove, beef

bovoletti/bovoloni, small snails in Venice

brace, alla, on charcoal

braciola (e), rib steak/chop/cutlet

braciola di maiale, pork chop

bracioletta, small slice of meat

bracioletta a scottadito, lamb chops (charcoal grilled)

bracioline/braciolone, meat roll

braciolone alla napoletana, breaded steak, rolled & stewed

branzino, bass. *Branzinotti* is small sea bass

brasato, braised/braised meat w/wine

bresaola, thinly sliced cured raw beef

briciole di pane, breadcrumbs

brioche, buns/rolls/small loaf (used for breakfast)

broccoletti, broccoli

broccoletti di rape, turnip greens

broccoletti strascinati, broccoli sautéed w/garlic & bacon

broccolo (i), broccoli

brodetto, rich fish soup

brodo, broth/soup/bouillon.
In brodo means cooked in broth

brodo di manzo, consomme/beef broth

brodo di pollo, chicken soup

brogue, sea bream

brovada, marinated turnips w/pork sausage

Brunello, full-bodied red wine from Montalcino

bruschetta, grilled bread w/garlic & olive oil (frequently
topped w/tomatoes &/or onions)

brut, very dry wine

brutti, small almond cakes

bucaniera, tomato & garlic seafood sauce

bucatini, hollow spaghetti noodles

bucatoni, same as *bucatini*, but larger

budino, custard/pudding

budino alla toscana, cream cheese w/raisins, almonds, sugar & egg yolks

bue, beef

burrata, a very buttery cheese found in Apulia

burrida, fish stew or casserole. In Sardinia this refers to a poached & marinated fish dish

burrini, a type of hard, aged cheese

burro, butter

burro maggiordomo, butter w/lemon juice & parsley

busecca, tripe & vegetable soup

buttiri, a type of hard, aged cheese

cacao, cocoa

alla cacciatora means in the style of the hunter

cacasor cioccolata, cocoa

cacciagione, game

cacciatora, alla/cacciatore, w/mushrooms, wine, tomatoes & herbs

cacciucco, spicy fish soup

cachi, persimmons

caciatella, a crème caramel dessert

cacio, *pecorino* cheese

caciocavallo, a hard, aged cheese made of whole milk

cacio e pepe, sauce made of black pepper & *pecorino* cheese

cacio e uova, w/cheese & egg

caciotta, mild cheese

caciucco, fish soup

caffè, coffee

Traditionally there must be as many types of fish in the soup as c's in cacciucco.

caffè al vetro, coffee served in a glass

caffè americano, American-style coffee (Italian coffee diluted w/hot water)

caffè con panna, coffee w/cream

caffè corretto, *espresso* w/a shot of liquor (usually brandy)

caffè doppio, coffee (a double serving)

caffè espresso, *espresso*

caffè freddo, iced coffee

caffè hag, decaffeinated coffee

caffè latte, coffee w/steamed milk

caffè lungo, coffee w/water (weaker coffee)

caffè macchiato, coffee w/a small amount of warm milk

caffè nero, black coffee

caffè ristretto, small, thick & strong coffee (stronger than an *espresso*)

calamaretto (i), small squid

calamari, squid

calamari fritti, fried squid

calamito, grey mullet

caldo (a)/caldi (e), warm or hot

caldaro, fish & potato soup

calzone (i), folded & stuffed pizza

cameriera, waitress

cameriere, waiter

camicia, in, poached

camomilla, camomile tea

camoscio, small deer (chamois)

campagnola, alla, w/vegetables & herbs

Campari, red aperitif w/a bitter, quinine taste

campo, del, wild. *Cicoria del campo* is wild chicory

candita (o), candied

canederli, dumplings made w/ham, sausage & breadcrumbs

canestrelli, sweet pastry/small sea snail or scallop

cannella, cinnamon

cannellini, small white beans found in Tuscany

cannelloni, large tube pasta stuffed w/fillings

cannelloni al forno, stuffed & browned in oven

cannelloni alla Barbaroux, stuffed w/ham, veal & cheese

cannelloni alla laziale, stuffed w/meat & onions

cannelloni alla napoletana, stuffed w/ham & cheese w/tomato & herb sauce

cannelloni alla piemontese, stuffed w/veal, ham & cheese

cannocchie, see *canoce*

cannoli alla siciliana, *ricotta* cheese-filled pastry w/sugar glaze

cannolicchio, razor-shell clam

cannolo (i), custard-filled pastry w/candied fruit or sweet white cheese (*ricotta*). This also refers to a short pasta tube

canoce, Venetian word for *cannocchie* which is neither a shrimp nor a lobster but something in between

cantarello, chanterelle mushroom

caffè.

Cantarello.

cantucci, almond biscuits

capelli d'angelo, thin noodle soup ("angel hair")

capellini, long, thin, fine spaghetti

capelunghe, razor clams

cape sante, scallops in Venice

capitone, large eel

capocollo, smoked pork salami

caponata, cold dish of eggplant & vegetables.
Eggplant, celery & onions are fried separately &
cooked in a sweet & sour sauce of raisins, tomatoes,
pine nuts, sugar & vinegar

caponata di melanzane, eggplant & pepper stew

cappelle di funghi, mushroom caps

cappelletti, rings of pasta filled w/ground meat.
Some think they look like little caps

cappello da prete, a triangular
sausage ("priest's hat")

cappero (i), caper

cappesante, scallops (means
"sacred shells")

capponcello ruspante al forno,
roast farm-raised capon

"Cappello da prete" means "priest's hat".

cappone, capon

cappon magro, vegetables & fish stacked high on a plate

cappuccino, coffee w/steamed milk

capra, goat

caprese, *mozzarella* & tomatoes. **Pasta caprese** is pasta
w/tomatoes, *mozzarella* & basil. *Caprese* means
from the island of Capri

capretto, baby goat

capretto al forno, roasted kid stuffed w/herbs

capretto alla pasqualina, roasted baby goat (an Easter dish)

capricciosa (o), chef's special (means "caprice" or "whim")

caprino, mild goat's-milk cheese

caprino fresco, a fresh goat's-milk cheese

caprino romano, hard goat's-milk cheese

capriolo, small deer (roebuck)

caraffa, carafe

caramellate, caramelized

caramella (e), candy (not chocolate)

caramello, caramel

carbonade, beef cooked in wine & onions

carbonara, pasta w/bacon (or ham), cheese, olive oil & eggs

carbonata, grilled pork chop. Sometimes this
refers to beef stew in red wine

carciofi alla giudea, deep-fried artichokes
(prepared in the shape of a rose).
This term means "Jewish-style artichokes"

carciofi alla romana, artichokes stuffed w/garlic, parsley &
mint, cooked in olive oil & white wine

carciofi in pinzimonio, raw artichokes in an oil dressing

carciofini in umido, artichole hearts sautéed in garlic & tomatoes

carciofini sott'olio, artichokes in olive oil

carciofino (i), small artichoke

carciofo (i), artichoke. The bottoms of artichokes are the *fondi
di carciofi*

Carciofo.

cardo (i), cardoon, a vegetable that looks like celery
but tastes like artichokes

carne, meat

carne a carrargiu, spit-roasted meat

carne cruda all`albese, slices of raw steak

carne di cervo, venison

carne macinata, ground meat

carne per arrosto in pentola, pot roast

carne tritata, ground meat

carone, large white beans

carota (e), carrot

carpa/carpione, carp

carpaccio, thinly sliced raw beef w/sauce. Named by the owner
of Harry's Bar in Venice after a famous Venetian painter

carpaccio di branzino, slices of raw sea bass w/a sauce

carpione, in, served cold w/vinegar sauce

carrargiu, spit-roasted

carré, sliced bread ("square")

"Carré" means square.

carrè di..., roast loin of... *Carrè di agnello* is rack of lamb

carrello, al, served from the food cart

carrettiera, tuna, garlic & pork sauce

carruba, carob

carta, menu

carta da musica, flat, crispy bread of Sardinia. See *pane carasau*

carteddate/cartellate, fried pastry dipped in honey

cartoccio, al, roasted (often in a paper bag, foil or other
covering). The covering is opened at the table

carvi (grani di), caraway (seeds)

casa, house. *Della casa* means "house specialty"

casalinga (o), homemade

cascà, the Sardinian version of couscous

casoncelli, pasta stuffed w/ground meat

cassata, ice cream (or sweet *ricotta* cheese) w/candied fruit

cassata alla siciliana, *ricotta* cheese-filled layered cake
w/sugar glaze

cassata gelata, various flavors of ice cream w/candied fruit

casserola/casseruola, casserole

cassoela/cassoeula, pork casserole

castagna (e), chestnut

castagnaccio, chestnut cake

castagnole, chestnut fritters

castellana, stuffed veal cutlet

Castelli Romani, white table wine
from the area southeast of Rome

Cavoletti.

castrato, mutton

catalogna, a type of salad green (like spinach, often cooked)

cauladda, Sardinian soup of cabbage, beans, sausage & meats

cavalla, mackerel. Also refers to a female horse

cavatappi, tubular pasta in the shape of a corkscrew

cavatelli/cavatieddi, homemade pasta

caviale, caviar

caviale del sud, "caviar of the south." Calabrian dish of dried
small fish preserved in oil & powdered w/*peperoncino*

cavoletti, Brussels sprouts

cavolfiore, cauliflower

cavolini di Bruxelles/cavoli di Brusselle, Brussels sprouts

cavolo (i), cabbage

cavolo broccoluto, broccoli

cavolo riccio, kale

cavolo rosso, red cabbage

cavolo verde, green cabbage

*EELS BREED in
fresh water &
mature in the
sea.*

cazzoeula, pork casserole

cecatelli, homemade pasta

cece (i), chickpea/garbanzo

ceche, baby eels

ceci alla Pisana, chickpea stew

cedrata/cedro, a large fruit that resembles a lemon.
The peel is used for flavoring

cee alla Pisana, baby-eel dish from Pisa

cefalo, grey mullet

cena, dinner

*cena —
chain-ah*

cenci, fried pastry
Centerbe, green herb liqueur
cèpes, porcini mushroom
Cerasella, cherry liqueur
cereale, cereal
cerfoglio, chervil
cernia, grouper
Certosino, green or yellow herb liqueur.
  This is also the name for a soft & mild cheese
cervella, brains
cervo, venison
cestino di frutta, a basket of fruit
cetriolino (i), pickle
cetriolo (i), cucumber
cevapcici, grilled meatballs found near Italian/Slovenian border
charlotte, spongecake & whipped-cream dessert
Chianti, well-known medium-bodied red wine from Tuscany.
  Chianti Classico comes from the center of the Chianti
  region, is aged for at least one year & is more complex.
  Riserva denotes a *Chianti* aged for at least two years
chiare, egg whites
Chiaretto, young & popular rosé wine
chicche, small potato *gnocchi*
chifferi, "c"-shaped tubular pasta
chiocciola (e), snail/sea shell-shaped pasta
chiocciolina, little snail
chiocciolini, spiral-shaped buns
chiodi di garofani, cloves
chiodino (i) a type of mushroom
chiodo di garofano, clove
ciabatta, large, coarse bread loaf
ciauscolo, soft, fatty pork sausage
cialda (e), waffle/wafer
cialledda, vegetable soup w/bread, olives, tomato, hard-boiled
  eggs & olive oil. A specialty in Basilicata
cialsons/chialzons, sweet & sour pasta
ciambella/chiambella/ciambelline, donut (not fried like North
  American donuts)
cibo, food
cibreo, chicken-liver dish
cicale di mare, type of shrimp (this crustacean is found off the
  coast of Italy. The name means "grasshopper")

Cenci ~
cHenchi

Cervella.
No grazie!

cicchetti/cicheti, snacks served in Venice. Similar to *tapas*
cicina, mixture of small fried fish
cicoria, chicory/endive
ciliegia (e), cherry
cima, stuffed veal served cold
cima alla genovese, veal stuffed w/mushrooms & sausage
cimalino, *cima* served w/beans. *Cimalino di manzo* is stuffed
    breast of beef
cime di rape, turnip greens
cinese, Chinese
cinghiale, wild boar
Cinque Terre, a dry, light white wine from the spectacularly
    beautiful five towns on the western coast of Italy
cioccolata, chocolate
cioccolata calda, hot chocolate
cioccolato, chocolate (hot chocolate)
ciociara, a seasoned meat sauce
cioppino, fish stew (this word is usually used only in
    the United States)
cipolla (e), onion
cipollina (e), chive
cipolline novelle, green onions
cipollotti, spring onions
ciriola, small eel
ciuppin, thick fish (& vegetable) soup
civraxin, Sardinian large bread loaf
cocco/noce di cocco, coconut
cocktail di vongole, clam cocktail (clams, olive oil & lemon)
cocomero, watermelon
cocozelle, zucchini
coda, tail
coda alla vaccinara, oxtail stew in a
    tomato & garlic sauce
coda di bue, oxtail
coda di rospo, monkfish
coglioni di mulo, finely ground pork sausage threaded with a
    wide strip of lard. The name means "mule's balls"
cognac, cognac
colazione (prima), breakfast
collo, neck
colomba, dove-shaped cake. *Colombo* means pigeon
colombacchi, wild pigeon

Cocomero.

coltello, knife

composta, stewed fruit (compote)

composta cotta, mixed cold, cooked vegetables

con, with

conchiglie, shell-shaped pasta. *Conchigliette* is a small version
used in soup

condimento (i), condiment

confetti, sugared almonds (used in weddings & special occasions)

confettura, jam

con ghiaccio, on the rocks

coniglio, rabbit

coniglio all'agro, rabbit stewed in red wine

coniglio all'Anconetana, a stuffed-rabbit dish

cono, cone (as in ice cream cone)

con seltz, w/soda

Coniglio.
Co-NEE-LEO

conserva, preserves/jam/jelly

conserva di frutta, preserves/jam/jelly

consommè, consomme (clear soup)

consommè madrilena, clear tomato soup

consommè reale, chicken consomme

contadina, alla, usually means served in a
tomato & mushroom sauce (means "peasant woman")

conto, check/bill

contorno (i), side dish/garnish. This often refers
to a vegetable side dish

contrafiletto/controfiletto, sirloin

copata, honey & nut wafer

coperto, cover charge

coppa, cup/goblet/small bowl.
Coppa can also refer to smoked
ham or smoked bacon

coppa di frutta, fruit cup/fruit cocktail

coppa di gamberetti, shrimp cocktail

coppa gelato, cup of ice cream/sundae

coratella di abbacchio, lamb heart, lung & liver dish

corda, lamb-tripe dish

cordulla, Sardinian dish made w/intestines

coregone, a type of salmon

coriandolo, coriander

cornetti, string beans

cornetto, croissant

corona, large white bean

Cornetto means trumpet.

49

corposo, full-bodied wine

corretto, coffee or *espresso*
    w/a shot of alcohol

Cortese, dry white wine

Corvo, dry, light white wine from Sicily

cosce di rana, frogs' legs

coscetta, leg/drumstick

coscia, leg

cosciette di rane, frogs' legs

cosciotto, leg

cosciotto di agnello, leg of lamb

cosciotto di porcello, leg of young lamb

costa, rib/scallop

costa di manzo, rib roast/T-bone steak

costa di sedano, celery stalk

costarelle di abbacchio a scottadito, grilled lamb cutlet

costarelli, spareribs/pork chops

costata, chop/beef steak. *Costata di vitello* is a veal chop.
    Costata di manzo is rib steak

costata alla fiorentina, grilled beef steak

costata alla pizzaiola, braised beef steak in a tomato sauce &
    mozzarella cheese

costate, rib steaks

costate d'agnello, rack of lamb

costatella, rib steak

costellata/costelleta/
    costelletine, rib steak

costicini, pork spareribs

costine, pork spareribs

costola arrostita, rib roast

costolatura, beef loin

costole di manzo, prime rib

costoletta (e), cutlet/chop (often coated in eggs & breadcrumbs
    & fried in butter)

costoletta alla bolognese, breaded veal cutlet w/tomato sauce,
    cheese & ham

costoletta alla milanese, breaded & fried veal cutlet

costoletta alla parmigiana, cutlet breaded & baked w/
    parmesan cheese

costoletta alla siciliana, thin slices of veal or beef topped
    w/chopped garlic & *parmesan* cheese, breaded & deep-fried

costoletta alla valdostana, cutlet w/ham & cheese stuffing

We have found that European cuts of meat often look nothing like cuts of the same name in the States.

costoletta alla viennese, wiener schnitzel
costoletta di vitello impanata, breaded veal cutlet
costolette di tonno, tuna steaks
costolette di vitello, veal chops
costolettine, lamb or pork chop
cotechino/coteghino, spicy pork sausage
cotognata, quince marmalade
cotogne, quince
cotoletta (e), cutlet, usually a veal cutlet
cotoletta alla bolognese, breaded veal cutlet topped w/ham,
  cheese & tomato sauce
cotto, cooked
cotto antico, bay leaf-flavored salami
cotto a puntino, medium done
courgette, zucchini
cozza (e), mussel
cozze alla marinara, mussels in white wine, garlic & parsley
cozze Posillipo, mussels in a spicy tomato sauce
crauti, sauerkraut
crema, cream/custard
crema caramella, custard w/caramelized-sugar topping
crema da montare, whipping cream
crema di, cream of
crema di funghi, cream of mushroom soup
crema di piselli, cream of pea soup
crema di pollo, cream of chicken soup
crema di verdura, puree of vegetables
crema fritta, fried-custard dessert
crema inglese, custard w/stewed fruit or cake
crème caramel, caramel custard
cremini, a type of mushroom
cremino, ice cream bar/a soft cheese
cren, horseradish
crescenza, a soft, buttery cheese (w/relatively low fat content)
crescionda, Umbrian dessert made from amaretto cookies,
  eggs, milk & unsweetened cocoa
crescione/crescione di fonte, watercress
crespelle, crêpes
crespelle alla fiorentina, spinach crêpes
crespolino, meat-filled pancake
croccheta (e), croquette
crocchette di patate, potato croquettes

Courgette is actually a french word found on menus near the french border.

crocchette di riso, deep-fried rice balls w/cheese in the center

crosta, crust (as in a pie crust)

crostaceo (i), shellfish

crostata, open-faced pie

crostata di frutta, fruit pie

crostini/crostoni, bread, fried or toasted in oil & topped
w/many ingredients/croutons

crostini alla napoletana, toast w/cheese & anchovies

crostini alla provatura, toasted diced bread
w/*provatura* cheese

crostini di mare, shellfish on fried bread

crostini di milza, toast w/veal paté

crostini Fiorentina, toast w/liver paté

crostini in brodo, croutons in broth

crostone di polenta, roasted meat (usually game) served on a
round base of *polenta*

crudo, raw

crusca, bran. This also refers to a bread found in Ticino w/
thick crust & dusted w/flour

cubbaita, nougat w/almonds, honey & sesame seeds

cucchiaio, spoon

cuccia, layered dish of slow-roasted meats, tomato sauce &
grains. A specialty in Calabria

cucina, cuisine

culaccio, rump meat

culatello, ham cured in white wine

cumino, cumin

cunillu, Sardinian word for rabbit

cuoco, chef

cuore (i), heart

cuore di sedano, celery heart

cuori di carciofi, artichoke hearts

curry, curry

cuscusu di Trapani, couscous

Cynar, after-dinner drink made of artichokes

daino, deer

da portar via, to go

datteri di mare, mussels

dattero (i), date

decaffeinato, decaffeinated

del giorno, of the day

della casa, of the house

[handwritten note:] "Cucina" means kitchen and cooking

[handwritten note:] "Decaffeinato" is becoming more common but be prepared for a condescending smile.

dente, al, pasta cooked until it's still slightly firm
(means "to the tooth")

dentice, a Mediterranean fish (dentex) similar to sea bream

denti d'elefante, tubular pasta (like *macaroni*)
(means"elephant's tooth")

di, of

diavola/diavolicchio, usually means served w/pepper or chili
peppers. Can also mean a dish cooked over a flame since
the terms mean "devil"

digestivo, after-dinner drink

diavolo-devil

disossata, boned rib steak

di stagione, in season

ditali, small tubular pasta for soup,
often called thimbles. ***Ditalini*** is the
smaller version of this pasta

diverso, varied

dolce (i), dessert/sweet/pastry. ***Dolce*** can also mean sweet wine

Dolcetto, fruity, dry red wine from Piedmont

dolci di Taglierini, sweetened noodle (taglierini) cake

dolcificante, artificial sweetener

dorato (a), browned/golden brown

Doria, alla, w/cucumbers

dragoncello, tarragon

e, and

e means and.
é with an accent
means is.

eliche, spiral pasta.
Often refered to as propellers

elicoidali, tubular pasta w/straight edges

emmenthal, Swiss cheese

empanata, breaded

entrecìte/entrecote di bue, boneless rib steak

erbazzone, vegetable pie

erbe, herbs

erbette, cooked greens

espresso, *espresso* (strong, small coffee)

espresso doppio, a double serving of *espresso*

espresso macchiato, *espresso* w/a small amount of foamy milk
on top. Compare this to ***latte macchiato***

Est Est Est, a dry, semi-sweet white wine

Etna, red & white Sicilian wines

etto, fish dishes are frequently served by the *etto*
(or 100 grams)

fagianella, bustard (bird)

fagiano, pheasant
fagioli al fiasco, slow-cooked Tuscan bean dish served
    w/garlic, herbs & olive oil
fagioli alla maruzzara, beans in an oregano & tomato sauce
fagioli all'Uccelloto, white beans in a tomato sauce
fagioli bianchi, white beans
fagioli bianco di Spagna, lima beans
fagioli cannellini, small white beans
fagioli con le cotiche, beans in a tomato sauce w/slices of pork
fagioli cotti al forno, baked beans
fagioli freschi, fresh beans
fagioli lessati al forno, boiled baked beans
fagioli lessi, shelled, boiled beans
fagiolino (i) green bean/French bean
fagioli rampicanti, runner beans
fagioli rossi, red kidney beans
fagioli sgranati, fresh shelled beans
fagioli toscani, cooked white-bean dish
fagioli verdi, green beans
fagiolo (i), bean
fagottini, food wrapped around a filling
Falerno, dry white & red wines
fame, hungry
faraona, guinea fowl
farcito (a), stuffed
farfalle/farfallette, bow-tie or butterfly-shaped pasta
farfalline (i), bow-tie or butterfly-shaped pasta
farina, flour
farinata, baked pancake made from olive oil, chickpea flour,
    salt & pepper (eaten as a snack)
farricello, barley
farro, a type of wheat, similar to spelt
farsumagru, veal or beef roll stuffed w/ham,
    bacon, cheese, onions & parsley.
    A Sardinian specialty
fasolini, scallops
fatto in casa, homemade
fava (e), broad bean. Sometimes called
    fave grande or *fave España*
favarella, bean soup
favata, bean, sausage & bacon casserole
fave al Guanciale, broad beans cooked w/bacon & onions

fagioli.

farfalle.

farricello.

fave e cicoria, pureéd fava beans, sautéed chicory &
olive oil. A specialty in Apulia

fegà, liver in Venice

fegatelli di maiale, pork liver

fegato (fegatini), liver.
Fegatini di maiale are pork livers;
fegatini di pollo are chicken livers

fegato alla veneziana, liver & onions

fegato di vitello, calf's liver

Fernet, a bitter digestive liqueur

ferri, ai, sliced & grilled (means "on iron")

fesa, leg of veal

fesa in gelatina, roast veal w/aspic jelly

fetta di/fette di, slice of...

fettina, small slice

fettuccine (i), long, flat, thin ribbon noodle

fettuccine Alfredo, thin ribbon noodles w/cream, butter & nutmeg

fettuccine alla Panna, thin ribbon noodles w/cream, butter &
nutmeg

fettuccine in brodo, noodle soup

fettuna, toasted or grilled over an
open fire w/garlic & olive oil

fettura di melacotogne, quince jam

fiamma, alla, flamed

fiammifero (i), match

fianco, flank

fiasco, straw-covered bottle

fichi d'India/fichi indiani, prickly pears

fichi in sciroppo, figs in syrup

fichi mandorlati, figs stuffed w/almonds

fico (fichi), fig

fidelanza, spaghetti in tomato
sauce in Liguria

filetti (di pomodoro), a sauce of sliced tomatoes

filetto (i), fillet or tenderloin

filu e ferru, Sardinian *grappa*

finferlo, an orange-colored mushroom

finocchiata, pork cured w/fennel & pepper

finocchio, fennel. *Finocchio selvatico* is wild fennel

finocchiona, fennel-flavored salami

fiocchetto, cold cut made from the leg of pork

liver in Venice,
liver in Milwaukee...
No grazie

fiasco. the old fashioned straw-covered bottle is really a novelty now.

fiocchi, flakes
fiocchi di granoturco, cornflakes
fiocco, ham shoulder
fior di latte, *mozzarella* made from cow's milk
fiore, flower
fiorentina, alla, w/oil, tomatoes & herbs
  (sometimes w/peas or spinach)
fiori con ripieno, stuffed zucchini flowers
fiori di zucca, zucchini flowers served either filled w/cheese,
  battered & fried or as a pizza topping
fiori di zucca fritti, fried zucchini flowers
flambé, flamed
focaccia, flat bread topped w/olive oil & sometimes cheese
  &/or onions. Can also mean cake
focaccia barese, stuffed pizza. A specialty of Apulia
focaccia di vitello, veal patty
foglia (e), leaf
foglia di alloro/foglia di lauro, bay leaf
foglia di vite, vine leaf
foiolo, tripe (stomach lining)
folpetto, the Venetian word for baby octopus
fondo di carciofo, artichoke heart
fonduta, melted cheese (fondue)
fontina, mild cheese (soft & creamy)
forchetta, fork
formaggini d'Alpe, cow's-milk cheese found in Ticino
formaggini di capra, fresh goat's-milk cheese found in Ticino
formaggio (formaggi), cheese
formaggio di fossa, aged sheep's-milk cheese
  from Le Marche
forno, al, baked
forte, strong
fracosta, rib steak
fragola (e), strawberry
fragole di bosco/fragoline di bosco, wild strawberries
fragolino, sea bream
fragolone, large strawberries
Frangelico, hazelnut-flavored cordial
frappé, milk shake
frascarelli, tiny *gnocchi*
Frascati, dry to slightly sweet white wine
frascota di bue, rib steak

foglia.

fragolone.

frattaglie, giblets
freddo (i)/fredda (e), cold/iced. *Tè freddo* is iced tea
fregolotta, flour, cornmeal & almond cake
fregula, dumpling soup
Freisa, dry to slightly sweet red wine
fresca (o), fresh/not cooked
freschi, wild mushrooms
fresco, al, outside (in the fresh air)
fricando, round of veal
fricassea, fricassee
fricò, cheese pancake
friggere, deep-fried (to deep fry)
frittata, omelette
frittata casalinga, plain omelette
frittata semplice, plain omelette
frittatina di patate, potato omelette
frittella (e), pancake/fritter
fritti ascolani, mixed fry of lamb chops, brains, olives
    & zucchini
fritto (a)/fritti (e), fried/deep-fried
fritto alla milanese, breaded & deep-fried
fritto alla napoletana, deep-fried fish, cheese & vegetables
fritto alla romana, deep-fried sweetbreads
fritto di verdura, fried vegetables
fritto misto, mixed deep-fried fish, meat or vegetables
fritto misto alla Fiorentina, meat & vegetable fritters
frittura, frying/fry
frittura del paese, mixed floured & fried seafood
frittura di pesce, mixed dish of fried small fish, squid &
    shrimp
frizzante, semi-sparkling wine
frolla, tender (meat)/flaky pastry
frollini, biscuits
frullato, milk shake
frullato di frutta, fruit milk shake
frumento, wheat
frumentone, corn
frutta, fruit
frutta candita, candied fruit
frutta cotta, stewed fruit
frutta fresca, fresh fruit
frutta secca, dried fruit

Freschi –
FRESS - KEE

frizzante.

frutti di bosco, berries
frutti di mare, seafood/seafood salad
fundador, w/brandy
funghetti, small mushroom-shaped pasta for soup
funghetto, al, sliced mushrooms cooked in garlic,
    onions & herbs
funghi trifolati, mushrooms sauteed in butter & garlic
fungo (funghi), mushroom
fuoco dell'Etna, strong, red Sicilian liquor
fusi, leg. *Fusi di pollo* is a chicken leg
fusilli, spiral-shaped pasta.
    Fusilli corti are short & *fusilli lunghi* are long
fusto, shank
galatina (in gelatina), pressed meat in aspic
galantina tartufata, truffles in aspic jelly
galletta, cracker/cookie. Can also refer to a mushroom or grape
galletto, chicken (cock)
Galliano, herb liqueur (yellow in color)
gallina, chicken (hen)
gallinaccio, woodcock/chanterelle mushroom
gallina faraona, guinea fowl
gallinella, waterfowl
gallinella faraona, guinea fowl
gallo, John Dory fish in Sicily
    (a firm-textured, white-fleshed
    fish w/a mild, sweet flavor
    & low fat content)
gallo cedrone, grouse (a game bird)
gamba, leg/drumstick/shank
gamba di vitello, veal shank
gamberelli, shrimp
gamberetta di rana, frogs' legs
gamberetto (i), shrimp
gambero (i), prawn/crayfish
gamberoni (gamberetti), large prawn
ganocchio, type of prawn
garetto, beef shank
garganelli, handmade pasta which is a square rolled into a tube
    (the dough is made from eggs, flour, grated *parmigiano*
    & nutmeg)
garofolato, beef stew
gaspaccio, gazpacho (the cold, tomato-based Spanish soup)

galletto.

gasata/gassata, carbonated
Gattinara, full-bodied red wine
gelatina, jelly/gelatine
gelato (i), ice cream/iced dessert
gelato al tartufo, ice cream w/chocolate sauce
gemelli, pasta made of two strands twisted
    around each other. The term means "twins"
genovese, alla, w/herbs
    (especially basil), olive oil
    & garlic/w/meat & onions
germe di grano, wheat germ
germinus, almond-meringue cookies
    from Sardinia

Genovese basil is considered the most fragrant.

germogli, sprouts
gesuita, rib steak
ghiacciato, chilled/iced
ghiaccio, ice
ghianchetti, small anchovies
ghiotta, alla, grilled or roasted
ghiozzo, mackerel

gesuito means Jesuit... presumably because the priests got the best meat.

giallo d'uova, egg yolk
gianchetti, small anchovies
gianduia, chocolate & hazelnut ice cream
gianduiotti, hazelnut-and-chocolate candies
giambonette(i)/giambonetto, boned chicken roll w/filling
giardiniera, small pieces of vegetables (a garnish)
gigantoni, large tubular pasta (means "giant")
gioddu, yogurt in Sardinia
giorno, del, of the day
gin, gin

Good Guess!

ginepro, juniper berry
ginestrata, chicken & sweet wine soup (a sweet & sour soup).
    A Tuscan specialty
girarrosto, spit-roasted
girasole, sunflower
girello, rump
glassate, glazed

girasole means turns to the sun.

gnoccata al pomodoro, tomato pizza
gnocchetti, small *gnocchi*
gnocchetti alla Sarda/gnocchetti sarda, small pasta
    dumplings in various sauces. A specialty in Sardinia
gnocchi, flour or potato dumplings

gnocchi alla marchigiana, *gnocchi* w/chicken-giblet sauce
gnocchi alla piemontese, little balls of flour, egg & potato
gnocchi alla romana, semolina (flour) dumplings
gnocchi di patate, little balls of potato, flour & egg
gnocco fritto, deep-fried rolls of pasta
gnocco ingrassato, *focaccia* w/prosciutto
gnudi, means naked (w/out pasta). Stuffing
    only, such as in *ravioli gnudi*
gnumariddi, a sweetbread dish
gomiti, "c"-shaped tubular pasta
gomma da masticare, chewing gum
gorgonzola, creamy, blue cheese (best-known Italian blue)
goulasch, goulash
graffo (i), doughnut
grana, mild, hard cheese (similar to *parmesan*)
granatina, steak tartare (raw ground beef). In most parts of
    Italy this term means Italian ice or shaved ice
granceola, spider crab. A specialty of Venice
granchio (di mare), crab
granciporro (i), crab
grande, large
granello, seed
gran farro, wheat & bean soup. Also see *farro*
grani di, seeds of...
granita, coffee or fruit syrup served over crushed ice
    (a "snow cone"). Originally made from snow from Mt. Etna
grano, wheat/corn
grano duro, duram wheat
grano padano, buttery, hard, seasoned cheese
    w/a grainy texture
grano saraceno, buckwheat
granoturco/granturco, corn on the cob
granseola, a crab found in Venice
grappa, liquor made from grape pressings.
    It's extremely strong
grappolo, a bunch
    (as in a bunch of grapes)
grassi vegetali, vegetable oil
grasso (a), oily/fatty/fat/grease
graticola, grilled/broiled
gratin/gratinate, oven-browned w/cheese
gratinada, baked dish topped

[handwritten notes:]
gnudi... don't pronounce the G. NOO.DEE
Kinda cute, hey?
Grappa is a popular digestivo which can taste like heaven... or hell.

w/grated cheese & breadcrumbs

gratis, free

grattugiato, grated

gratuito (a), free

gremolata, minced anchovies, parsely & lemon (used as a garnish)

grenadine, veal chunks (used in casserole dishes)

gricia, alla, w/bacon, onion, cheese & chili pepper

griglia, alla, grilled (usually charcoal grilled)

grigliata mista, mixed grill of meats or fish

Grignolino, high-quality red wine

grissino (i), long, thin bread stick

grongo/gruonco/grangu, conger eel

groppo, rump (meat)

groviera/groviera svizzera, sharp
cheese w/holes (like Swiss cheese)

guancia.

guancia, pig's cheek. *Al guanciale* means cooked w/bacon &
onions. Also refers to the delicacy of pig's cheek

guardaroba, coat room

guarnite, alla, served w/a garnish

guazzetto, usually refers to a stew (meat or fish). In Sardinia,
this dish almost always contains capers

gubana, sweet bread roll (dried fruit & nut strudel found in
Friuli-Venezia Giulia)

gulyas, beef stew found in Friuli-Venezia Giulia

gusti, flavors

hasce di manzo, hamburger patty

igname, yam

impanato (a), covered in breadcrumbs

impazzata di cozze/impepata di cozze, mussels cooked in
their own juice w/black pepper, oil, parsley & garlic

incapriata, purée of fava beans & chicory

incasciata, layered dough, meat sauce, hard-boiled eggs, cheese

incluso (a), included

Indiana, all', w/curry (Indian style)

indivia, endive/chicory

indivia Belga, Belgian endive

insaccati, salami

insalata, salad

insalata all'americana, shrimp & mayonnaise salad

insalata caprese, tomatoes, basil & *mozzarella* salad.
Originally a specialty on the island of Capri, but now
found everywhere in Italy

insalata cotta, cold, cooked vegetable salad *insalata cotta...* *love it!*
insalata di campo, field lettuce
insalata di cesare, Caesar salad
insalata di crudita, mixed raw vegetable salad
insalata di frutti di mare, seafood salad
insalata di funghi, raw mushroom salad
insalata di mare, seafood salad
insalata di patate, potato salad
insalata di petti di pollo, chicken salad w/walnuts
insalata di tonno, tuna salad
insalata di verdura cotta, boiled vegetable salad
insalata mista, mixed salad
insalata riccia, curly endive
insalata russa, diced potato & vegetable salad w/mayonnaise
insalata siciliana, salad featuring fennel & black olives
insalata verde, green salad
integrale, whole wheat
involtini al sugo, rolled veal cutlets w/ham & cheese & topped
    w/tomato sauce
involtini di cavolfiori, cabbage leaves stuffed w/meat
involtini di pesce, thin fish slices stuffed w/*prosciutto* & herbs
involtini di salvia, a deep-fried sage-leaf anchovy roll
involtini di vitello, veal roll usually stuffed w/salami & cheese
involtino (i), stuffed roll
iota, hearty vegetable soup (white beans, cabbage & bacon fat).
    A specialty of Trieste
Ischia, an island at the north end of the Gulf of Naples
I.V.A., abbreviation for Value Added Tax (V.A.T.)
jota, thick bean & sauerkraut soup (see Iota)
julienne, small strips of vegetables
kirsch, al, w/a clear cherry brandy
knoedel/knödeln, dumplings found in the *Krapfen...* *sounds good!*
    Trentino-Alto Adige region
krapfen, doughnuts (Austrian name)
laccetto, mackerel
lacerto, mackerel
Lacrima Christi, popular red, *Lacrima Christi -* *tears of Christ*
    white & rosé wines
Lago di Caldaro, light red wine
Lagrein Rosato, rosé wine
Lambrusco, well-known red wine (sweet)
lamelle di fegato, thin slices of liver sautéed in butter

lampasciuni, wild onions
lampone (i), raspberry
lampreda, lamprey (similar to an eel)
lanzado, mackerel

Lampreda.
Non grazie!

lardarellatta alla fiamma, larded & cooked on a grill
lardo, bacon/salt pork/lard
lardone, salt pork
lardoons, cured & fried pork
lardoso, meat fat
lasagne, thin layers of dough & meat, tomatoes, cheese &
  sauce (baked in the oven)
lasagne al forno, large strips of pasta cooked in sauce
lasagne alla portoghese, baked custard caramel
lasagne alla vincisgrassi, baked *lasagne* w/meatballs
lasagne verdi, spinach *lasagne*
latte, milk
latte al cacao, chocolate milk
latte di mandorla, almond milk
latte intero, whole milk
latte macchiato, steamed milk w/a small amount of *espresso*.
  Compare this to ***espresso macchiato***
latte magro, skim milk
latterini, poached fish dish
latte scremato, skim milk
latticini, small *mozzarella* balls
lattonzolo, suckling pig
lattuga (e), lettuce
lattuga romana, romaine lettuce
lauro, bay leaf
lavarello, a type of salmon
laziale, alla, w/onions
lecca-lecca, sucker/lollypop
leccia, pompano
leggero, light or weak/light wine
legume (i), vegetable
lenticchia (e), lentil
lepre, hare
lepre in salmì, marinated hare ("jugged hare")
leprotto, young hare
lessato (a), boiled
lesso, boiled. This can also refer to meat or fish stew
letterato, small tuna fish

Latte.
generally not
drunk by
the glass.

limonata.

lievito, yeast/baking powder
lievito di birra, brewer's yeast
limonata, lemonade/lemon soda
limoncello, alcohol & lemon-zest drink. This is
    called *limoncino* in the Cinque Terre
limone (i), lemon. *Al limone* means w/lemon juice
lingua, tongue
linguine, flat noodles
liquore (i), liqueur. *Liquore Strega* is a sweet herb liqueur
liquoroso, fortified dessert wine
liscia/lisce, refers to smooth pasta (w/out ridges)
liscio, straight. *Brodo liscio* is plain broth
lissa, pompano in Venice
lista, menu. *Lista dei vini* is the wine list
livornese, alla, usually beans in tomato sauce w/celery
    & onions
locale, local
lodigiano, a type of *parmesan* cheese
Lombarda, alla, served fried in butter w/lemon juice & parsley
lombata, loin/leg. *Lombata di maiale* is a pork chop. *Lombata*
    di vitello is a grilled veal chop
lombata ai sassi, floured steak sautéed in butter w/sage & fried
    potatoes
lombatine, tenderloin or cut of meat for filet mignon
lombello, loin/leg
lombo di manzo, beef loin/sirloin
lombo di vitello, veal sirloin
lonza, loin
lucanica, spicy sausage
lucerna (e), grouper
luccio, pike

Lumaca.

lucullo, alla, raw beef (steak tartare)
Lugana, dry white wine
luganega, pork sausage. This spicy sausage from Basilicata
    has many similar spellings such as *luganica* & *lucanica*
lumaca (lumache), snail. *Lumache* also refers to snail-shaped
    pasta. *Lumachine* is a small version of this pasta
    used in soup
lumache alla Bourguignonne, snails w/garlic butter
    ("Burgundy snails")
lunga, long (as in long pasta or *pasta lunga*)
lungo, lighter *espresso*

lupo di mare, sea perch

luvasu, sea bream

maccarello, mackerel

maccarones con bottarga, Sardinian pasta w/fish eggs

maccaruni di casa, Sicilian pasta dish served
w/tomato & meat sauce

maccheroni, *macaroni*

maccheroni al pettine, pasta w/ridges usually served w/ragù

macchiato, *espresso* w/a small drop of milk

macco di fave, broad bean, onion & tomato soup

macedonia di frutta, fruit salad

macedonia di legumi, mixed cooked vegetables

macinata, ground. *La carne macinata* is ground beef

madera, al, cooked in Madeira wine

mafaldine, pasta ribbons

maggiorana, marjoram

magro, dish w/no meat/lean.
Ravioli di magro is stuffed pasta
w/herbs & *ricotta* cheese

marjoram is a member of the oregano family.

maiale, pork

maionese, mayonnaise

mais, corn

malfatti di ricotta, *ricotta gnocchi. Malfatti* means badly
made, a reference to the handmade dumplings in this dish

malloreddus, flavored dumplings found in Sardinia

malloreddus all'oristanese, saffron-flavored dumplings w/a
sauce of Swiss chard, cream & eggs

maltagliata, *macaroni*

mammole, artichokes *Mammole.*

mancia, tip

mandarino (i), tangerine/mandarin

mandorla (e)/mandorlata, almond

manicotti, stuffed (w/cheese & meats), baked pasta dish

mantecato, whipped ice cream. This also refers to a way to
prepare cod

manzo (di bue), beef

manzo arrosto ripieno, stuffed roast

manzo lesso, boiled beef

manzo salato, corned beef

manzo stufato al vino rosso, beef stewed in red wine

maraschino/marasco, w/Maraschino (cherry-flavored liqueur)

marchigiana, alla, a dish in the style of Le Marche (one of the regions of Italy), usually cooked w/chicken giblet sauce

mare, di, of the sea

mare-monti, a dish served w/mushrooms & shrimp

margarina, margarine

margherita, this term is used to describe a pizza w/tomato, *mozzarella* & basil

marinara, alla, usually, but not always, means in tomato sauce (usually w/garlic & onions). The term means "of the sea" or "sailor's style," so can also refer to a dish w/seafood

marinata (o), marinated

maritozzo, soft bread roll

marmellata, marmalade/jam

marmellata d'arance, marmalade

marrone (i), chestnut. *Marrons glaces* are candied chestnuts

Marsala, fortified dessert wine from Sicily

marsala, al, in a Marsala (fortified dessert wine) sauce

Martini, vermouth

mascarpone, a soft, very creamy, fresh cheese (even for cheese, it's high fat)

masenette, tiny crabs eaten whole (w/the shell)/Venetian word for small soft-shelled crabs

matriciana, bacon, tomato & spices sauce

mattone, al, pounded flat (usually chicken) & roasted in a brick oven

mazza da tamburo, a parasol-shaped mushroom

mazzancelle/mazzancolle, very large prawns

mazzancougni, very large prawns

medaglione, medallions

medallione, a grilled ham & cheese sandwich

media, medium

mela (e), apple

melacotogna, quince

melagrana, pomegranate

melanzana (e), eggplant

melanzane al funghetto, sautéed eggplant

eggplant is a member of the same family as tomatoes, potatoes & peppers.

melanzane alla Napoletana, eggplant Neopolitan style (layered w/cheese & tomato puree & baked in an oven)

melanzane alla parmigiana, eggplant *parmesan* (w/tomatoes & *parmesan* cheese)

melanzane ripiene, stuffed eggplant

melassa, molasses

meliga, cornmeal

melone, melon/canteloupe
menta, mint
mentine, mints
menù, menu
menù a prezzo fisso, set menu
menù turistico, fixed-price menu
merca, roast fish dish from Sardinia
merenda, late morning/afternoon snack
meringa, meringue
meringa chantilly, meringue shells filled w/whipped cream
meringato/meringhe/meringua, meringue
merlango, hake/cod/whiting
merlano, whiting, cod or hake
merluzzo, cod
messicani, veal scallops dish/veal rolls
mesticanza, mixture of salad greens
metà, half
mezzo (a), half
mezzelune ai pinoli, pine-nut cookies from Umbria
mezze maniche, short tubular pasta
miascia, bread & fruit pudding
midollo, marrow
miele, honey
miglio, millet

millefoglie means a thousand leaves

milanese, alla, battered w/eggs & breadcrumbs & fried
Millefiori, herb-based liqueur
millefoglie, puff pastry/napoleon
millerighe, ridged tubular pasta (means "thousand lines" after the ridges in the pasta)
mimosa, spongecake & whipped-cream dessert
minerale, mineral (as in *acqua minerale* or mineral water)
minestra (minestre), soup (usually thick soup)
minestra al farro, soup made with *farro* (a wheat similar to spelt)
minestra di cipolle, onion soup
minestra di fagioli, bean soup
minestra di farina tostata, toasted-flour soup
minestra di farro, soup made with *farro* (a wheat)
minestra di funghi, cream of mushroom soup
minestra di lenticchie, lentil soup
minestra di pomodoro, tomato soup
minestra di riso, rice soup

minestra in brodo, broth w/noodles or rice & chicken livers

minestra maritata, meat broth & vegetable soup

minestre di piscialetto, dandelion-greens soup

minestrina, soup (usually clear)

minestrone, bean & vegetable soup w/noodles, vegetables, rice

minestrone alla genovese, vegetable soup
w/*macaroni* & spinach

minestrone verde, thick vegetable soup w/herbs & beans

mirabella (e), small plum

mirtillo (i), blueberry. The word *mirtilli* is also used for berries
in general & for cranberries

mischianza, salad of wild greens, herbs & edible flowers

misoltini, salted & dried shad (fish)

misticanza, salad of wild greens, herbs & edible flowers

misto/misti, mixed

misto del golfo/misto del paese, mixed floured & fried seafood

misto mare, mixed floured & fried seafood

mitilo, mussel

moka, mocha

molto, very

montanara, alla, has many meanings but generally means
w/red wine sauce or w/vegetables

montare, to whip (usually refers to cream)

montebianco/Mont Blanc, pyramid of sweetened chestnuts &
whipped cream (named after Mont Blanc)

Montepulciano, full-bodied, dry red wine

montone, mutton

monzittas, snails in Sardinia

mora (e), blackberry

Mont Blanc is the French side of Monte Bianco mountain.

mormora, small fish found in the Mediterranean

mortadella, luncheon meat w/pistachio nuts & peppercorns

morto, pot roast

mosca, con la, a drink (usually *Sambuca*) served "w/the
fly"(*con la mosca*). The "fly" is a coffee bean in the glass

moscardino (i), small squid

Moscatello/Moscato, muscatel (table & dessert white & red
wines from the muscat grape)

mostarda, mustard. This word is rarely used. Most use *senape*

mostarda di frutta, candied fruits in syrup/preserved fruits in
a mustard sauce/fruit chutney

mousse al cioccolato, chocolate mousse

mozzarella, a soft, fresh (unripened), slightly sweet cheese

mozzarella di bufala, *mozzarella* made from buffalo milk
mozzarella in carrozza, fried *mozzarella* sandwich
    (means "in a carriage")
muddica, breadcrumbs in Sicily
muggine, grey mullet
muscoletti, shank
muscoli, mussels. This word is rarely used. Most use *cozze*
muscoli alla marinara, steamed mussels dish
musetto, salami
napoletana, ("Naples-style") w/tomato sauce (w/out meat)
nasello, whiting/hake/cod
naturale, plain/natural
nave, di, w/seafood
navone (i), turnip
`nduja, Calabrian pork sausage
Nebbiolo, full-bodied dry red wine
nepitella, an herb similar to mint
nero (a), black
nervetti, calf's foot dish (tendons of calves' feet).
    A Venetian specialty
nespola, medlar (a tart fruit)
nidi di rondine, pasta rolls
nocciola (e), hazelnut
noccioline americane, peanuts
nocciole, nuts
noce (i), nut/walnut. Can also refer to the top round of veal
noce di cocco, coconut
nocelli, walnut-raisin cookies
noce moscata, nutmeg
nocepesca, nectarine
noci d'anacardo, cashews
Nocillo/Nocino, liquor made from walnuts
nodino (i), chop/small grilled pork chop
non, not
non fumatori, no smoking
non gassata, still or not carbonated
nonna, alla, this can be any sauce served w/pasta. The term
    means "grandmother" & there are as many variations of
    "alla nonna" as there are grandmothers
norcina, sausage & cheese sauce. After the town of Norcia
Norma, alla, this usually refers to a dish served w/eggplants,
    tomatoes, basil & sometimes *ricotta* cheese

Navone.

nervetti...
I don't
think so.

nostrale/nostrano, home-grown/local

novellame, a spread of salted anchovies & *peperoncino* sauce

novello/novelli, fresh/tender

o, or

oca, goose

occhiate, orata (a fish)

occhi di lupo, small tubular pasta
   "wolves' eyes")

olio, oil/olive oil

olio d'arachide, peanut oil

olio da tavola, salad oil

olio di cartamo, safflower oil

olio di girasole, sunflower oil

olio di grano/olio di granturco, corn oil

olio di palma, palm oil

olio di semi, seed oil/corn oil

olio d'oliva, olive oil

olio santo, chili-infused oil

oliva (e), olive (*nere*, black, *verdi,* green)

olive agrodolci, olives in sugar & vinegar

olive ascolane, large green olives. *Olive all'ascolana,*
   in Le Marche, olives stuffed w/meat & fried in olive oil

ombra, glass of wine in Venice. This word is usually used at a
   bar & not at a restaurant

ombrina, umbrine (seafood/bass)

omelette, omelette

omelette casalinga, plain omelette

omelette semplice, plain omelette

oranciata, orangeade

orata, a fish found in the Mediterranean (bream/gilthead)

oratino, a small *orata* fish

orecchiette, small ear-shaped pasta

orecchiette con le cime di rapa, small ear-shaped pasta
   w/turnips. A specialty in Apulia

origano, oregano

ortaggi, vegetables/greens/herbs

Orvieto, light, dry, white wine from Orvieto in Umbria

orzata, almond or barley-flavored water

orzetto, barley & potato soup

orzo (i), rice-shaped pasta. Can also refer to barley

osso, bone

ossobuco (ossibuchi), braised veal-shank dish. You may be

*Olio d'oliva
we never leave
Italy without
a bottle*

given a marrow spoon to eat the marrow in the bone

ossobuco alla milanese, veal shank, tomatoes, garlic & wine

ostrica (ostriche), oyster

ovalina, a type of *mozzarella* cheese

ovolo (i), a rare (& delicious) mushroom w/an orange & scarlet color. Sometimes called Caesar's mushroom

pacchetto, package

paciugo, parfait

padella, in, fried

paesana, alla, usually means served w/bacon (or sausage), potatoes, carrots & other vegetables

paeta, spit-roasted turkey

pagaro/pagello, sea bream/porgy

paglia e fieno, pasta dish w/yellow (egg) & green (spinach) pasta (means "straw & hay")

pagliarino, soft, mild cheese

pagliata, a dish containing organ meat

pagnotta, loaf

pagnotta del cacciatore, game birds roasted in dough

pagro, sea bream/porgy

paiata, spit-roasted turkey

paillard, beef rib steak or veal cutlet pounded thin & grilled

pajata, a dish containing organ meat

palamito, bonito fish

palemone, prawns

pallina, scoop (as in scoop of ice cream). The word really means "marble"

palomba/palombaccia, pigeon

palombacci, an Umbrian dish of small birds cooked whole on a spit

palomba.

They're all over the down place.

palombo, dogfish/shark found in Sicily

panafittas, dried bread broken into pieces & boiled (like pasta), then served in a tomato sauce in Sardinia

panardo, a thirty-course feast served in Abruzzo

panata, bread soup

pancetta, bacon (cured pork belly)

pancetta arrotolata, rolled bacon flavored w/cloves

pan có Santi, sweet bread w/raisins, dates, honey & walnuts. "Saints' bread" is eaten around All Saints Day (November 1)

pan di Genova, almond cake

pan di Spagna, spongecake

pandolce, cake w/dried fruit

pandoro (di Verona), star-shaped light cake w/sugar topping

pane, bread/loaf

pane bianco, white bread

pane bigio, whole-wheat bread

pane carasau, flat crispy bread found in Sardinia. Also known
as *carta da musica* (music paper)

pane di segale, rye bread

pane e coperto, the charge for bread & for sitting at the table

pane frattau, *pane carasau* topped w/tomato sauce, grated
cheese & a fried egg. A specialty in Sardinia

pane grattugiato, breadcrumbs

pane integrale, whole-wheat bread

panelle, chickpea fritters

pane nero, dark bread

pane pepato, gingerbread

pane piccante, gingerbread

pane scuro, pumpernickel bread

pane toscano, sourdough bread

pane tostato, toast

panettone, spiced cakes or
coffeecakes w/candied fruits

Pane. The Italians, like the French, are fiercely proud of their bread.

panforte, flat, hard fruitcake

pan grattato, breadcrumbs

panicielli d'uva passula, grapes wrapped in leaves & baked

panino (i), roll/sandwich

panino imbottito, sandwich

paniscia, rice, sausage & bean soup

pan matteloch, honey bread found in the lake country

pan meino, cornmeal bread/cake (millet bread) w/elderflowers

panna, cream

panna, alla, served in a cream sauce or w/creamy gravy

panna, con, in a cream sauce/w/cream

panna cotta, rich cream custard

panna da montare/panna montata, whipped cream

pannocchia, corn on the cob

panpepato, gingerbread or hazelnut cake

pansoti/pansotti, triangular-shaped filled pasta

pan tostato, toast

panzanella, bread & vegetable salad

panzerotti, baked (or deep-fried) dough filled w/pork, cheese, tomatoes or other ingredients

panzoni, stuffed ravioli dish

paparot, cornmeal & spinach dish from Friuli-Venezia Giulia

pappa al pomodoro, tomato & bread soup

pappardelle, long, flat, wide pasta

pappardelle al sugo di lepre/pappardelle alla lepre, strips of
    pasta w/rabbit sauce

paprica, paprika

pardulas, Sardinian pastries filled w/cream cheese

parigina, hamburger buns. In Sicily, this refers to bread

parmigiana, alla, w/*parmesan* cheese & tomatoes

parmigiana di melanzane, baked slices of eggplant layered
    w/*parmesan* cheese, tomatoes & *mozzarella*

parmigiano, *parmesan* cheese usually served grated

parmigiano-reggiano, the "real" name for *parmesan* cheese

partenopea, means "Naples' style," the same as ***Napolitana***

Pasqualina, "Easter style" which can mean roasted in an oven
    w/olive oil, onion, garlic, black olives & celery. ***Torta***
    Pasqualina is a pie featuring artichokes

passate di legumi, puree of vegetables

passatelli, pasta of *parmesan* cheese, eggs & breadcrumbs

passato, puree

passato di verdura, cream of vegetable soup

passera di mare, flounder

passera pianuzza, flounder

passerino, flounder

pasta, pasta (dough made of
    flour, oil, butter, eggs & water).
    The first course in Italy. If you find
    -*ette* or -*ini* after pasta, this means a smaller version of
    pasta. For example, *pennette* & *pennini* are smaller versions
    of *penne*. If you find -*oni* after pasta, this means a large
    pasta like *rigatoni*. *Pasta* that starts w/*taglia* is made of
    long, thin strips. *Pasta* can also mean pastry

pasta al forno, any pasta mixed w/a sauce & baked

pasta alla Norma, pasta w/tomatoes, basil & eggplant topped
    w/*ricotta* cheese

pasta asciutta, any pasta not eaten in soup

pasta con le sarde, pasta w/fresh sardines

pasta d'arachide, peanut butter

pasta di olive, olive paste

pasta e ceci, pasta & chickpea soup

pasta e fagioli, pasta & bean soup
pasta frolla, puff pastry
pasta in brodo, pasta in broth
pasta 'ncasciata, pasta baked w/eggplant, salami, tomato/basil
pasta reale (paste reali), marzipan cake
   (means "royal pastry")
pasta sfoglia, puff-pastry dough
paste, pastries
pastella, batter for frying
pasticceria (e), pastry
pasticcetti, small tarts
pasticciata, baked pasta (in a casserole)
pasticcini da te, teacakes/small pastries
pasticcino (i), cake/small pastry/tart
pasticcio, pastry/pie. Also the Venetian word for baked lasagne
pasticcio di maccheroni, sweet pie containing meat sauce
pastiera napoletana, *ricotta* cheese-filled pastry
pastina, small pasta usually used in soup
pastina in brodo, pasta served in soup
pastissa, pot pie
pasto, meal
patata (e), potato
patate al lesso, boiled potatoes
patate al ghiotto/patate alla ghiottona, stuffed baked potatoes
patate americane, sweet potato
patate arroste, roasted potatoes
patate bollite, boiled potatoes
patate dolci, sweet potato
patate fritte, fried potatoes/french fries
patate in padella, potatoes fried in a pan
patate lesse, boiled potatoes
patate novelle, new potatoes
patate rosolate, roasted potatoes
patate saltate, potatoes sliced & sautéed
patate tenere, new potatoes
patatine fritte, french fries/chips
patatine novelle, small roasted potatoes
pate/paterini, pâté
pecora, sheep/ewe
pecorino, hard, sharp cheese usually served grated.
   Pecorino alla griglia is a Sardinian specialty of grilled
   pecorino cheese

[handwritten note:] anti - before / pasto - meal / antipasto.

pellegrine, scallops
penne, tube-shaped pasta (cut at an angle)
pennette, smaller version of *penne*
penneziti, larger version of *penne*
pennoni, the largest version of *penne*
peoci, mussels. Also the Venetian word for "head lice"
pepata di cozze, mussels in a black pepper, oil & garlic sauce
pepato, peppered
pepe, black pepper
pepe di Giamaica, allspice
peperonata, tomatoes, peppers & onion stewed together
peperoncino (i), small, spicy pickled pepper
peperone (i), pepper
peperoni alla brace, roasted marinated peppers
peperoni imbottiti, stuffed peppers
peperoni ripieni, stuffed peppers
peperoni rossi, red peppers
peperoni sott'aceto, pickled chilis
peperoni verdi, green peppers
pera (e), pear
perciatelli, hollow spaghetti noodles
per contorno, meal includes salad or side dish
pere helene/pere elena, poached pear served in vanilla ice
   cream & topped w/chocolate sauce
pernice, partridge
persico, perch
pesca (pesche), peach
pesca melba, peaches in syrup w/ice cream & whipped cream
pescatora/pescatore, seafood sauce for pasta & rice dishes
pescatrice, angler fish
pesce, fish
pesce carpionata, marinated fish in herbs
pesce in saor, fish in a sauce of onion, raisin, pine nut &
   vinegar. A specialty in Veneto
pesce persico, perch
pesce San Pietro, John Dory fish (a firm-textured, white-
   fleshed fish w/a mild, sweet flavor and low fat content)
pesce sciabola, an eel-like fish
pesce serra, bluefish
pesce spada, swordfish
pesce stocco, cod
pesce turchino, mackerel

pesche, peaches
pesche aurora, spongecake soaked in peach liqueur
pesto, basil, oil, garlic & pine-nut sauce
petonchio, scallops
petroniana, alla, can mean many things, most frequently
    breaded & fried & topped w/melted cheese
pettine (i), small scallop
petto, breast (of poultry)
petto alla principessa, chicken floured & fried in butter &
    served w/an egg on top
petto all'arancio, chicken in an orange sauce
petto di pollo, chicken breast
peverada, chicken liver & anchovy sauce *only for the brave.*
pezzenta, pork salami
pezzo, piece
piacere, of your own choice (your pleasure)
piadina, soft, flat bread
pianuzza, flounder/halibut
piastra, grilled on a flat steel plate
piattino, saucer
piatto (i), dish/plate. *Piatti freddi* means cold dishes
piatto del giorno, dish of the day
piccante, highly seasoned (hot)
piccata (e), veal scallop
piccata all'allegro, veal scallop fried in butter w/lemon juice
piccata alla Lombarda, veal scallop fried in butter w/lemon
    juice & parsley
piccata di vitello, veal cooked in lemon & parsley
piccatina, veal scallop dish
piccioncino, young pigeon
piccione, pigeon
piccione selvatico, wild pigeon
piccolo (i)/piccola (e), small
pici, eggless pasta
piede (i), foot
piemontese, sauce w/truffles ("Piedmont style")
pietanza, dish/main course
pignata, lamb or goat w/herbs. A specialty from Basilicata
named after the terra-cotta pot it's cooked in
pimento, pimento/allspice
pimiento, sweet red peppers
pinoccate/pinocchiata, almond & pine-nut cake

pinolata, pine-nut dessert cake found in Tuscany

pinolo (i), pine nut

Pinot Grigio, light, fruity white wine

pinsimonio/pinzimonio, oil, pepper & salt dressing/oil & mustard dressing for dipping

pinza, yellow flour, pine nut & raisin cake from Veneto

pipe, pasta similar to *lumache* (a snail-shaped pasta)

pisello (i), pea

pistacchi, pistachio nuts

pitta, pizza either stuffed or topped with many ingredients. Popular in Calabria

piviere, plover (bird)

pizza, pizza

pizza alla marinara, the "true" pizza: tomato, olive oil & oregano

Pizza... Man's highest culinary achievement.

pizza alla napoletana, pizza w/cheese, capers, tomatoes, anchovies, olives & *mozzarella*

pizza alla siciliana, pizza w/salami or ham, anchovies, olives, tomatoes & *mozzarella*

pizza bianca, pizza bread topped w/sea salt & olive oil

pizza capricciosa, same as *pizza quattro stagioni*

pizza di Pasqua, cheese bread

pizzaiola, w/tomato & garlic sauce

pizzaiolo, pizza man (the maker of pizzas)

pizza margherita, pizza w/tomato, basil & *mozzarella*

pizza marinara, pizza w/garlic, oil & oregano. Can also refer to a pizza w/black olives, anchovies, tomatoes & capers

pizza quattro stagioni, w/seafood, cheese, artichokes & ham in four sections. Means "four seasons" & is a pizza which has a different topping for each quarter

pizza rustica, common in central Italy; serves large rectangular pizzas with thicker crusts and more toppings than usually found in a *pizzeria*. You can order as much as you want, and pay by weight

pizzelle, small (fried) pizzas

pizzetta, small pizza

pizzoccheri, pasta made w/buckwheat flour

polenta, cornmeal mush

polenta concia, *polenta* w/cheese

polenta di grano saraceno, buckwheat *polenta*

polenta dolce, sweet *polenta* dessert

polenta e osei, *polenta* w/roast fowl

polenta grassa, butter, fontina cheese & *polenta*

polenta pasticciata, *polenta* served w/meat sauce, cheese, mushrooms & sauce (*polenta* pie)

polipetto (i), small squid/baby octopus

polipo (i)/polpo (i), octopus

pollame, poultry

pollastra/pollastrello, young chicken

pollo al mattone/pollastrino al mattone, chicken pounded flat & roasted in a brick oven

pollo al mattone is a favorite!

polletto, spring chicken

pollo, chicken

pollo alla diavola, highly spiced, grilled chicken

pollo alla Marengo, sautéed chicken dish with many ingredients (usually tomatoes, mushrooms & onions). The dish takes its name from the town of Marengo, where Napoleon defeated the Austrians

pollo alla romana, fried chicken pieces, bacon & garlic

pollo all'arrabbiata, "Enraged chicken" (a spicy chicken dish)

pollo arrosto, roasted chicken

pollo fritto Fiorentina, chicken marinated in oil, lemon juice & herbs

pollo in bellavista, roasted chicken dish w/vegetables

pollo novello, spring chicken

pollo piccata al Marsala, chicken pounded thin & fried in butter & Marsala wine

pollo scarpariello, boneless chicken w/lemon, garlic & parsley

polpa, lean meat/flesh

polpetielle, baby octopus

polpetta (e) di carne, meatball

polpetti affogati, small octopuses cooked w/tomatoes (means "drowned octopuses")

polpettine (i), meatball. *Polpettine di pesce* is a seafood ball

polpettone, meat loaf

polpi arricciati, "curled octopus." An octopus dish in which the octopus is curled by beating & twirling it in a basket

polpo, octopus

polpo in purgatorio, octopus sautéed in oil w/tomatoes & peppers

pomi d'oro, the original name for tomato (means "golden apple"). It's believed that the tomato arrived in Europe w/a golden color that turned red under the hot

Mediterranean sun
pommarola (salsa di), tomato sauce
pomo (i), apple
pomodoro (i), tomato
pomodoro, al, w/tomato sauce
pomodoro doppio (concentrato), thick tomato paste
pomodoro pelati, peeled tomatoes in their own juice
pomodoro pumate, sun-dried tomato
pomodoro super cirio, thick tomato pureé
pomodori con tonno, tomatoes stuffed w/tuna
pomodori secchi, sun-dried tomatoes
pompelmo, grapefruit
popone, melon
porcecellino, suckling pig
porceddu/porcheddu, Sardinian word for roast suckling pig
porcello, young pig
porchetta, roast suckling pig stuffed w/herbs
porcini, mushrooms (the wild mushroom boletus)
porco, pork
porri dorati, battered & deep-fried leeks
porro (i), leek
portacenere, ashtray
portafoglio, veal cutlet stuffed
    w/herbs, cheese & other ingredients.
    This is also the word for wallet

porta cenere Can't get away from it in Italy.

portata (e), course
porto, port
portoghese, usually means
    w/tomato sauce
porzione, portion
posillipo, seafood sauce
praio, dorade (fish)/gilt-head bream
pranzo, lunch/dinner
presnitz, dessert made w/dried fruit from
    Fruili-Venezia Giulia
prezzemolo (i), parsley
prezzo, price
prezzo fisso, fixed price
prima colazione, breakfast
primavera, spring vegetables & cream sauce
primizie, spring vegetables or fruit
primo, first (as in ***primo piatto,*** first course)

principale, main (as in *piatto principale*, main course)
profiterole, filled ice-cream puff topped w/chocolate sauce &
   whipped cream
prosciutto, aged & cured ham
prosciutto affumicato, cured, smoked ham
prosciutto cotto, cooked or boiled ham
prosciutto crudo, salted, cured ham/Parma ham
prosciutto di cinghiale, smoked wild boar
prosciutto di San Daniele, a cured ham
   named after a town in the Friuli-Venezia Giulia region
prosciutto e melone, ham & melon
prosciutto di Parma, Parma ham
   (famous cured ham of Parma)
Prosecco, sparkling white wine from Veneto
provatura, soft, mild & sweet cheese
provenzale, onions, black olives, tomato & mushroom sauce
provolone, mild buffalo cheese
provolone dolce, mild, white, medium-hard cheese
provolone piccante, sharp cheese
prugna (e), plum
prugna secca (prugne secche), prune
pumaruolo/pumaruoro, tomato in Sicily & Campania
pumate, sun-dried tomatoes
punta di vitello, veal brisket
puntarelle, a salad green
punte di asparagi, asparagus tips
Punt e Mes, orange-flavored vermouth
   (drunk before meals)
puntino, a, medium done
punto, breast. *Punto* also means medium rare
purea, pureed/mashed
purea di fave, a puree of broad beans
   often spread on bread
purè di patate, mashed potatoes
puttanaio, a stew-like ratatouille
   (means "prostitute stew")

Absolute favorite

puttanesca, tomato, black olives, anchovies, capers & garlic
   sauce (the term means "prostitute"). Allegedly named
   because prostitutes could prepare this quick meal between
   "customers"
quadrello, pork loin
quadrello d'agnello, rack of lamb

quadretti, refers to small squares of pasta
quadrucci, square-shaped pasta for soup
quaglia (e), quail
quattro formaggi, four cheeses
quattro spezie, four spices combined
   (pepper, cloves, juniper & nutmeg)
quattro stagioni, pizza
   w/seafood, cheese,
   artichokes & ham
   in four sections

Quattro Stagione means Four Seasons

rabarbaro, rhubarb. This can also refer to an
   after-dinner liqueur
radiatori, pasta shaped like a radiator
radicchio, red endive/red chicory (bitter red lettuce)
rafano, horseradish
ragnetto, rolls
ragno, sea bass
ragno di mare, spider crab
ragù, tomato-based meat sauce
ragusano, hard, slightly sweet cheese
ramolaccio, horseradish
ranapescatrice, angler fish
rane, frogs or frogs' legs
rannocchi, frog or frogs' legs
rapa (e), turnip
rape rosse, beet root

Rana.

raspante, farm-raised (usually chicken). Means "scratching"
Ratafia, black-cherry liqueur
rattatuia, ratatouille
ravanada, horseradish sauce
ravanello (i), radish
raviggiolo, goat's-milk cheese
ravioli, squares of pasta w/stuffing. *Raviolini* are half-circle
   stuffed pasta
ravioli gnudi, ravioli stuffing (without the pasta)
ravioli verdi, spinach ravioli
razza, ray
recchie/recchietelle, the word in Apulia for *orecchiette* (ear-
   shaped pasta)
remolazzitt, radish
rene (i), kidney
ribes, currants

ribes neri, black currants

ribes rossi, red currants

ribollita, vegetable soup (which means "reboiled") thickened w/bread. There are many versions of this Tuscan soup

ricciarelli, marzipan &/or almond biscuits

riccio (di mare)/ricci (di mare), sea urchin

ricciola, amberjack (fish)

riccioli, small, curly pasta

riccolo, curly endive

Ribollita means Reboiled.

ricotta, similar to cottage cheese, sweetened when used in desserts

ricotta al maraschino, *ricotta* cheese w/maraschino

rigaglia (e), giblets

rigata (e), refers to ridges in pasta

rigatoni, large tube-shaped pasta (always has ridges)

rigatoni alla Norma, a Sicilian dish of pasta w/eggplant & tomato sauce

righini, bluegill

ripieno/ripiene, stuffed

riserva, mature wine

risi e bisi, creamy rice w/green peas. *Bisi* is the Venetian word for peas

Risi e Bisi... another favorite.

riso (i), rice

riso ai gamberi, rice w/shrimp

riso alla genovese, rice w/sauce of minced beef (or veal) w/vegetables

riso alla Greca, rice, vegetables & sausage dish (Greek style)

riso alla milanese, golden rice dish from Milan featuring saffron

riso alla pilota, rice w/a sausage meat sauce

riso e ceci, broth of rice & chickpeas w/tomatoes & spices

riso in bianco, white rice w/butter

riso in cagnone, boiled rice topped w/*parmesan* cheese

riso mantecado, rice cooked in butter & milk

riso nero, black rice. The rice is made black from squid ink

risoni, rice-shaped pasta for soup

risotto, creamy rice dish w/various ingredients. Served as a first course, *i primi*, after the *antipasto*

risotto ai fiori di zucca, rice dish made w/a heavy cream base & zucchini flowers stirred in w/*parmesan*. A Ticino specialty

risotto alla certosina, creamy rice dish w/shrimp, mushrooms, peas & sometimes frogs' legs

risotto alla mantovana, rice dish w/salami & *parmesan* cheese

risotto alla milanese, rice w/butter, saffron, beef, zucchini & *parmesan*

risotto alla pescatora, spicy rice w/seafood

risotto alla romana, rice usually w/lamb & potatoes

risotto alla valdostana, rice w/cheese & wine

risotto alla Valenciana, the same dish as Spanish *paella*

risotto alla Veneta, rice w/mussels

risotto alla veronese, rice & ham w/mushrooms

risotto al salto, crisp rice cake

risotto di frutti di mare, rice w/shellfish

risotto di peoci, rice w/mussels

risotto nero, black *risotto*. Squid or cuttlefish ink makes the rice black

ristretto, reduced broth

robiola, soft, mild & slightly sweet cheese

robiolina, sheep's-milk cheese

rocciate, pastry w/fruit & nuts

rognoncini, kidneys

rognoncini al vino bianco, kidneys in white-wine sauce

rognone (i), kidney

rolatine di vitello, veal cutlets stuffed w/ham &/or cheese

rollè, roll

romagnola, typically, a sauce of tomato, garlic & parsley

romana, alla, a catch-all term that literally means "Roman style"

rombo, turbot

rosato, rosé

rosbif, roast beef

roscioli, red mullet in Abruzzo

rosé, rosé (blush) wine

rosmarino, rosemary

Rosolio, sweet liqueur

rospo, monkfish/angler fish. *Rospo* also means toad, so this fish is often referred to as *pesce rospo*

rosso, red

Rosso Antico, cherry-flavored vermouth

rotella, round

rotelle/rotelline, wheel-shaped pasta

rotini, spiral-shaped pasta

rotolo, rolled meat w/stuffing. *Rotolo di spinaci* is a spinach roll (pasta w/spinach)

rovi, blackberries

rucola, arugula, also called rocket salad

rughetta, salad green

rujolos, Sardinian sweet-cheese fritters

rum, rum

ruote di carro, pasta in the shape of a wheel (same as *rotelle*)

rustica, alla, usually means a pepper & olive sauce, but can mean many things

sagro, sea bream

salame (i), smoked sausage. *Salamino* is a small salami

salame di cioccolato/ salame al cioccolato, chocolate cake in the shape of (& looks like) a salami

salamino piccante, pepperoni

salatina, greens for salad

salatini, crackers/snacks

salato, salted/salami

salciccia, sausage

sale, salt

Salame! (handwritten)

salmi, in, marinated in wine, garlic & herbs (usually w/game)

salmone, salmon. *Salmoncino* is young salmon

salsa, sauce. *Salsa balsamella* is béchamel (white) sauce

salsa bianca, white sauce

salsa di pommarola, tomato sauce

salsa di salsiccie, sausage sauce

salsa per la cacciagione, "hunters' sauce" for cooking game

salsa tartara, tartar sauce

salsa verde, parsley-based green sauce (w/oil, lemon juice, capers & garlic)

salsicce di maiale, pork sausages

salsiccia (e), fresh sausage

saltato (i)/saltata (e), sautéed

saltimbocca, veal cutlet wrapped around ham & sage

Saltimbocca means jump in the mouth. (handwritten)

salumi, sausages

salumi cotti, cooked sausages & cured meats

salvia, sage

salvietta, napkin (paper)

Sambuca, anise-flavored liqueur. When served *con la mosca* ("w/the fly"), the "fly" is a coffee bean in the glass

sanato, young calf

sandwich, sandwich

sangiovese, primary grape of Chianti wine

sangue, al, rare

Sanguinaccio, blood sausage (black pudding).
 Also a chocolate spread made from chocolate & pigs' blood

San Pietro, John Dory fish (a firm-textured, white-fleshed fish
 w/a mild, sweet flavor and low fat content)

San Severo, dry red wine from southern Italy

saor, sweet & sour sauce

sapa, thick sauce made from the juice of freshly pressed grapes

saporito (a), mild/tasty

sarago (saraghi), bluegill

sarda (e)/sardine, sardine

Sarde.

sarda, alla, tomato & meat sauce w/herbs & red wine
 ("Sardinian style")

sarde a beccaficu, sardines usually stuffed w/pine nuts &
 raisins. A Sicilian specialty

sardella, fried baby fish minced w/olive oil & powdered
 peppers from Calabria

sardina, small sardine

sardo, hard, aromatic cheese

sardoncini, little sardines

sartù, baked rice dish w/tomatoes, meatballs & mushrooms

savarin, cake baked in a ring mold & soaked in liquor. The
 center is filled w/fruit & whipped cream

sbrisolona, flour, cornmeal & almond cake (crumble cake)

scalogno (i), shallot

scaloppa, veal scallop (thin slices of veal)

scaloppa alla fiorentina, veal scallop w/spinach & white sauce

scaloppa milanese, breaded, fried veal scallop

scaloppa napoletana, veal scallop coated in breadcrumbs

scaloppina (e), veal scallop

scaloppine alla boscaiola, veal scallops sautéed in oil & butter
 & served w/an herb, black olive & onion sauce

scaloppine alla campagnola, veal scallops served in a sauce.
 The term means "rustic"

scaloppine al marsala, small veal scallops in marsala wine

scaloppine al vino bianco, small veal scallops in
 white-wine sauce

scamorza, mild cheese (aged *mozzarella*)

scampi, shrimp/prawns

scampi all'Americana, shrimp in a tomato sauce

scanello, sirloin

scapece, fried fish in vinegar & saffron/fried vegetables which are then marinated

scarda, bream (fish)

scarola, escarole (a crispy leaf lettuce)

scarpaccia, zucchini pie (means "old shoe")

scarpena, scorpion fish

scelta, of your choice

schiacciata, flat bread (means "squashed flat")

schila, shrimp in Venice

schmarren, crêpes w/fruit & cream from Trentino-Alto Adige

scialatielli, wide noodles

scialcione, bread loaf

sciroppato (a), cooked in syrup

sciroppo, syrup

sciroppo d'acero, maple syrup

scodella, bowl

scorfano, scorpion fish

scorfano rosso, scorpion fish

scodella .

scorze d'amelle, pasta shaped like slivered almonds found in Basilicata

scorzonera, salsify

scotch, scotch

scottadito, grilled lamb chops

scottiglia di cinghiale, wild-boar chops

scrippelle, omelettes cut into thin strips & served in a meat broth. A specialty in Abruzzo & Molise

sebadas, bread filled w/cheese & honey, then fried. A Sardinian specialty

secco (a), dry. *Funghi secchi* are dried mushrooms

secondo piatto, second course

sedani, the name for a small pasta similar to *rigatoni*

sedano, celery

sedano rapa, celery root

segale, rye

sella, saddle

selvaggina, game/venison

semente/semenza/senze, seeds

semi di, seeds of...

semi di melone, pasta noodle for soup in the shape of melon seeds

semifreddi, (half-cold) desserts frozen or refrigerated before service

semigreggio integrale, semi-whole wheat rice

semolino, flour
semplice, plain
senape, mustard
senza, without
seppia (e), cuttlefish/squid
seppioline, small cuttlefish/squid
serpentone, pastry stuffed w/chopped figs, apples & nuts
servizio, service/service charge
servizio compreso, service included
servizio incluso, service included
servizio non compreso, service not included
servizio non incluso, service not included
sesamo, sesame
sete, thirsty
sevàdas, Sardinian deep-fried pastries
sfilatino, bread loaf
sfogie, Venetian word for sole
sfoglia/sfogliatella/sfogliatelli, flaky-crusted shell-shaped
    pastry filled w/sweetened *ricotta* cheese
sfogliata, flaky pastry
sfogliata di crema, cream puff
sformato, similar to a souffle
sfratti, sweet walnut rolls (a Christmas dessert)
sgavecio, pickled fish
sgombro (i), mackerel
sidro, cider
sigarette, cigarettes
silvano, chocolate tart
Silvestro, herb & mint liqueur
smacafam, *polenta* dish w/*asiago*
    cheese & sausage

Smacafam means hunger killer

Soave, slightly dry white wine from Veneto
sodo/sode, hard boiled
soffritto, sautéed/stock (the base for soup or the sauce for
    pasta) often made w/pigs' organs. Can also refer to slightly
    fried or browned onions, carrots & celery, a base for many
    dishes
sogliola, sole   *Sogliola so-LEE-oh-la*
sogliola all'Arlecchino, sole served w/a cream sauce
sogliola alla mugnaia, sole sautéed w/lemon, butter & parsley
sogliola margherita, sole covered w/hollandaise sauce
soia, soy

sopa, soup

sopa cauda, soup w/bread & roast pigeon

soppressa, sausage

soppressata, sausage/sausage made from pig's head

sorbetto, sherbet/sorbet

sorbetto al calvados, sherbet flavored w/apple brandy

sorrentina, often refers to a tomato, basil & mozzarrella sauce

sottaceti, pickles

sottaceto, pickled

sottoaceti, pickled vegetables/pickles

sottofiletto, beef or veal loin

sott'olio, in olive oil

sottonoce, top round of veal

Sotto aceti means under vinegar

spaccatina, bread loaf

spaghetti, spaghetti (long, thin pasta)

spaghetti aglio e olio, spaghetti w/olive oil & garlic

spaghetti alla bolognese, spaghetti w/meat sauce

spaghetti alla carbonara, spaghetti w/cream, bacon, cheese & egg

spaghetti alla checca, spaghetti w/raw tomatoes, basil & garlic

spaghetti alla gricia, spaghetti w/onions, bacon, pepper & grated cheese

spaghetti all'amatriciana, w/tomato sauce, cheese & garlic

spaghetti alle vongole, spaghetti w/clam sauce

spaghetti al ragù, pasta w/meat & tomato sauce

spaghettini, thin spaghetti

spaghetti pomodoro e basilico, spaghetti w/tomatoes & basil

spalla, shoulder

spanocci, very large prawns

sparaci, asparagus in Venice

sparnocci, type of shrimp

specialità della casa, specialty of the house

specialità di questa regione, specialty of the region

specialità di questo ristorante, specialty of the restaurant

specialità locali, local specialties

specialità regionali, regional specialties/local dishes

speck, cured ham found in the Trentino-Alto Adige region

spelt, a hard wheat

speziato, spicy

spezie, spice

spezzatino, meat or poultry stew/little pieces

spezzato, a stew

spicchio (d'aglio), clove (of garlic)
spiedini alla corsara flambe, grilled meat served "flaming"
spiedini di mare, pieces of grilled fish on a skewer
spiedino (i), any dish roasted on a skewer
spiedo, allo, on a spit
spiga di grano, ear of corn
spigola, sea bass/grouper
spinaci, spinach
spiza di grano, ear of corn
spremuta, fresh fruit drink
spugnola, morel mushroom
spuma, mousse
spumante, sparkling wine
spumone (i), ice cream w/candied fruit, nuts & whipped cream
spumoni al croccante, *spumoni* topped w/toasted,
    caramelized almonds
spuntatura, breast of...
spuntino, snack
stagionato (a), well aged
stagione (i), season (in season)
starna, a type of partridge
stecca di, bar of
stecchi fritti, fried kebabs
stecchino, toothpick/skewer
stellette/stelline, star-shaped pasta
stinchetti, marzipan cakes (in the shape of human bones)
stinco, braised veal or pork shank. The most common version
    of this dish is **stinco di maiale al forno,** a whole pork shank
    oven-roasted w/wine, garlic & rosemary
stoccafisso, dried cod
storione, sturgeon
stracchino, a soft, creamy white cheese
stracciate, scrambled eggs
stracciatella, egg-drop soup. This can also
    refer to chocolate-chip ice cream
stracotto, beef stew w/pork sausage/
    pot roast
strangolapreti, see *strozzapreti*
strangozze, see *stringozzi*
strapazzate, scrambled
strascinati, shell-shaped pasta
stravecchio, *parmesan* cheese aged at least three years

Stinco actually means shin bone.

Strega, a strong herb liqueur

strigghie, red mullet in Sicily

stringozzi, a homemade pasta from Umbria

strisce, ribbon noodles

strozzapreti, dumplings or
gnocchi w/meat sauce.

strudel, this famous pastry roll
can be found in
Trentino-Alto Adige

Strozzapreti means Priest stranglers. A gluttonous priest supposedly choked to death on one.

strutto, lard

stufatino, pot roast or stew

stufato, braised/stewed/stew

stuzzicadenti, toothpicks

stuzzichino (i), appetizer

succhi di frutta, sweetened
fruit juice

succo, juice

succo di frutta, fruit juice

succu tunnu, dumpling soup

Succu tunnu. Never had it but love the name.

sufflé, soufflé

sugna, lard

sugna piccante, a spicy sauce made from pork fat (added to
dishes in Basilicata)

sugo, sauce/gravy/juice

sugo, al, w/tomato sauce

suino, pork

suppli/suppli di riso, breaded & deep-fried rice balls usually
filled w/ham & cheese

suprema di pollo in gelatina, chicken breast in aspic

suro, mackerel

susina (e), plum

tacchino, turkey

tacchino
TA-KEE·NO

tagliata di manzo, grilled beef

tagliatelle, short ribbon noodles

taglierini, thin noodles

taglierini alla chitarra, a pasta dish featuring a sheet of pasta
cut w/a cutter called a *"chitarra"* or guitar

tagliolini, very narrow, thin flat noodles

tajarin, egg noodles found in Piedmont & Valle d'Aosta

taleggio, cheese w/a mild, buttery flavor

taralli, biscuits made in the shape of a ring

tartara, alla, raw w/lemon sauce

tartaruga, turtle

tartina (e), open-faced sandwich/tart.
  Tartine are often appetizers

tartufi di cioccolato, chocolate "truffles"
  (chocolate-coated ice cream)

tartufi di mare, small clams/cockles

tartufo (i), truffle (funghi that grows around tree trunks)

tartufo di gelato, ice cream w/chocolate sauce

tartufo nero, black truffle from Tuscany

tasse, taxes. Menus will often indicate if *tasse e servizio* (taxes
  & service) are included

tavola (o), table

tavola calda, snack bar/fast food

tavoletta di cioccolata, chocolate bar

tazza, cup

TAZZA di té.

tè, tea

tè cinese, Chinese tea

tè d'India, Indian tea

tè freddo, iced tea

tegamaccio, lake-fish stew from Umbria

tegame/tegamino, al, sautéed

teglia, alla, pan-fried

teglia di pesce spada, marinated swordfish dish

tellina (e), clam

teneroni, veal chops

terrina, tureen

testa, head. *Testa di vitello* is calf's head   *I'll pass.*

testina, head

testuggine, turtle

tiedde, fish casserole from Apulia

tiella, any dish with baked layers of ingredients

tiella di agnello, roasted lamb dish

tiella di riso e cozze, mussels, rice & potato dish found in
  Apulia

tigelle, flat bread

timbale/timballo, meat & vegetable casserole w/layers of pasta

timo, thyme

tinca (tinche), tench (seafood)

tiramisù, spongecake soaked in
  espresso & brandy w/cream &
  chocolate. *Marsala* can also
  be used in this
  delicious dessert

Tira misu made its way to Italy from the U.S.

91

tirolese, alla, usually means
w/fried onion rings

tisana, herbal tea

tisana al cinorrode, rose-hip tea

tisana al tiglio, lime tea

tisana camomilla, camomile tea

tocco di funghi, mushroom sauce

toc de purcit, pork stew w/white wine from
Friuli-Venezia Giulia

toma, sharp cheese

tomini, fresh cheese from Piedmont

tonarelli/tonarrelli/tonnarelli, thin string pasta

tondino, bread loaf

tonica, tonic water

tonnato, in a tuna sauce. Can also refer to a cold veal dish

tonnetto, small tuna

tonno, tuna

topinambur, artichoke
(Jerusalem artichoke)

tordo (i), thrush (a bird)

torlo, yolk

torrone, nougat

torta (e), tort/cake/pie

Torrone is immensely popular in Italy.

torta al pesto, spinach & cheese pie/flat
bread cooked over hot stones in Umbria
& filled w/cheese, meat or greens

torta di frutta, fruit tart

torta di gelato, ice-cream cake — *yes please.*

torta di mele, apple tart

torta di tagliatelle, egg-noodle cake

torta di verdure, sweet vegetable pie
(similar to American pumpkin pie)

torta gianduia, chocolate & nut cake

torta meringa, large meringue pie filled w/fruit & topped
w/whipped cream

torta millefoglie, napoleon (layers of pastry filled w/ice cream
or whipped cream & topped w/frosting)

torta Pasqualina, Easter puff-pastry cake

torta rustica, cornmeal-cake dessert

torta sbrisolona, flour, cornmeal & almond cake
(crumble cake)

torta tarantina, potato pie

torta turchesca, rice-pudding tart from Venice
torta zuccotto, liquor-soaked sponge cake filled w/ice
    cream or whipped cream, chocolate & candied fruits
tortelli di zucca, pasta stuffed w/pumpkin
tortellini, filled pasta rings
tortello (i), small doughnut/fritter
tortellone (i), a larger *tortellini* pasta
tortiera, cake/pie
tortiglione, almond cakes
tortiglioni, tube-shaped pasta (larger than *cannelloni*)
tortina di marmellata, jam tart
tortini di riso, rice cakes
tortino, tart/cheese & vegetable tart similar to quiche
tortino di carciofi, dish of fried artichokes & eggs
toscana, alla, w/tomatoes & herbs
tostato (a), toasted
totano (i), squid
tournedos, small tenderloin steaks
tovaglia, table cloth
tovagliolo, napkin

Tovagliolo

TOV-A-LEE-OH-LO

tozzetti, hazelnut & almond biscuits (flavored w/anise)
tracina dragone, a fish named "dragon" after its
    dangerous spines
tramezzino, small sandwich
trancia/trancio, piece/slice
trattaliu, cooked lamb intestines. A specialty in Sardinia
trenette, long, flat, thin ribbon noodles
trifolati, sliced mushrooms cooked in butter, garlic & oil
trifolato, w/truffles
triglia (e), red mullet
triglia alla Livornese, red mullet cooked w/tomatoes, garlic &
    parsley
trigoli, water chestnuts
trippa (e), tripe
trippa alla fiorentina, braised
    tripe & minced beef
    w/tomato sauce & cheese
trippa alla milanese, tripe
    w/onions, carrots, tomatoes,
    beans & leeks
trippa alla romana, tripe in a
    tomato & vegetable sauce

You can put all the "ALLA"s you want on trippa and it's still TRIPE.

tritato (a), ground (as in ground beef)

trofie, pasta similar to *gnocchi*

trombetta da morto, a type of mushroom

trota (e), trout

trota alle mandorle, stuffed-trout dish

trota di ruscello, river trout

trota iridea, rainbow trout

trota salmonata, salmon trout

trota spaccata, trout split in two, dipped in batter & deep-fried

trotella, trout

tuaca, a mixture of brandy, citrus fruits & herbs

tubetti, *macaroni*

tubi, refers to all tubular pasta

tuorlo, yolk

tutto compreso, all included

ua, grapes in Venice

ubriaco, cooked in red wine

uccelletti/uccelli, small birds (of
all kinds) usually spit-roasted

uccelletto, all', w/tomato sauce & sage. *Piselli all' uccelleto*
are peas cooked in tomato sauce w/sage

uccelli scappati, pork, pork sausage &/or small-bird kebabs

ueta, raisin in Venice

uliva, olive

umido, in, stewed

uopa, sea bream

uova, eggs

uova affogate, poached eggs

uova affogate nel vino, eggs poached in wine

uova à la coque, soft-boiled eggs

uova albume, egg whites

uova al burro, eggs fried in butter

uova al guscio, soft-boiled eggs

uova alla campagnola, eggs w/diced vegetables & cheese

uova alla coque, boiled eggs

uova alla fiorentina, fried eggs served on spinach

uova all'americana, fried eggs (usually served w/bacon)

uova alla russa, similar to deviled eggs

uova all'occhio di bue, fried eggs

uova al tegame con formaggio, fried eggs w/cheese

uova barrotte, soft-boiled eggs

uova bollite, soft-boiled eggs

94

uova frittata/uova fritte, fried omelette
uova frittata al pomodoro, tomato omelette
uova frittata al prosciutto, ham omelette
uova in camicia, poached eggs
uova molli/uova mollette, soft-boiled eggs
uova ripiene, stuffed eggs
uova semplice, plain omelette
uova sode agli spinaci, eggs florentine
uova tonnate, hard-boiled eggs in tuna sauce
uovo (a), egg
uovo fritto (uova fritte), fried egg
uovo sodo (uova sode), hard-boiled egg
uovo strapazzatto (uova strapazzate), scrambled egg
uva, grapes
uva bianca, green grapes
uva nera, black grapes
uva passa/uva passita, raisins
uva secca, raisin
uva spina, gooseberry
uvetta, white raisins
vaniglia, vanilla
valdostana, alla, usually means served w/ham & cheese
    (means "Valle d'Aosta style")
valigetta, roasted veal breast
Valpolicella, light (slightly bitter) red wine from Veneto
vapore, a, steamed
vario/vari, assorted
Vecchia Romagna, wine-distilled brandy
vegetable, vegetable
vegetariano (a), vegetarian
velluta, creamy soup
veneziana, alla, w/onions, white wine & sometimes mint
ventaglio, scallop
ventresca, white-meat tuna. Can also mean a boiled pork dish
verde, green/green pasta (w/a spinach base)
verde in pinzimonio, vegetable dip
Verdicchio, a dry white wine from Le Marche
verdura (e), green vegetable
verdura trovata, sautéed wild greens w/potatoes
verdure cotte, cooked vegetables
vermicelli, thin, long spaghetti noodles
vermut, vermouth

verza, cabbage

verzelata, grey mullet

vincigrassi/vincisgrassi, baked lasagna dish. Named after an
   Austrian prince, this dish is a specialty in the region of Le
   Marche where it's usually served w/chicken-giblet sauce

vincotto, a spread made from grapes

vinello, light wine

vino (i), wine

vino amabile, sweet wine

vino asciutto, very dry wine

vino bianco, white wine

vino brut, very dry wine

vino corposo, full-bodied wine

vino da pasto, table wine

vino da tavola, table wine
   (the lowest-quality wine made
   from any combination of grapes)

amabile also means loveable which pretty much refers to all wine as far as we're concerned.

vino del paese, local wine

vino dolce, sweet wine

vino frizzante, sparkling wine

vino leggero, light wine

vino nostrano, local wine

vino novello, new wine

vino rosatello, rosé wine

vino rosato, rosé wine

vino rosé, rosé (blush) wine

vino roseo, rosé wine

vino rosso, red wine

vino da tavola is low quality wine but not necessarily bad.

Vin Santo/Vinsanto, dessert wine from Tuscany & Trentino

vino secco, dry wine

vino semi secco, semi-sweet wine

vino spumante, sparkling wine

vino tipico, local wine

violino, cured leg of goat

visciola, wild cherry

vitellini, very young veal

vitello, veal

vitello all'uccelletto, diced veal & sage simmered in wine

vitello tonnato, cold veal w/tuna sauce

vodka, vodka

vol-au-vents, filled pastry shells

vongola (e), small clam

You weren't really looking this up were you?

vongole, alle, in a clam sauce

vongole oreganate, clams baked or broiled w/oregano

vongole veraci, small clams boiled in vinegar,
   hot pepper & garlic

whisky, whiskey

wurstel, hot dogs (similar to smoked hot dogs)

yogurt/yoghurt, yogurt

yogurt magro, low-calorie yogurt. *Yogurt intero* is not low-fat

zabaglione/zabaione, custard dessert flavored w/Marsala

zafferano, saffron

zalettini, shortbread cookies from Venice *I'll pass.*

zampa (e), pig's (or beef) feet

zampetto, pork leg

zampone, large pig's foot scraped clean of its insides & then
   stuffed w/spicy sausage

zampone di maiale, stuffed pigs' feet

zelten, dried fruit & nut cake from Trentino-Alto Adige

zenzero, ginger

zèppola, doughnut/fritter *— Sì, grazie!*

zesti, orange or lemon peel (can also be candied)

ziba, fragrant herb from Sardinia

zimini, in, cooked w/vegetables. *In zimino* can refer to spinach
   or Swiss chard stewed w/cod or squid & tomatoes

zimino, Sardinian fish stew

zingara, alla, "Gypsy style." Each chef has his or her own
   version of this sauce of many ingredients

zite (i), narrow, hollow-tube pasta

zucca, pumpkin or squash

zucca ovifera, squash

zucchero, sugar

zucchero a velo, powdered sugar

zucchero a zollette, lump sugar

zucchero greggio, brown sugar

zucchero grezzo, brown sugar

zucchero in pezzi, lump sugar

Zuchino
ZOO·KEEN·E

zucchero in polvere, powdered sugar

zucchine al burro versato, zucchini w/black-butter sauce

zucchine farcite, zucchini filled cheese, ham & mushrooms

zucchine fritte, deep-fried strips of zucchini

zucchine scapecce, pieces of zucchini fried in oil w/garlic

zucchine trifolate, sliced zucchini in butter, parsley & garlic

zucchino (i), zucchini

zucchina (e), zucchini
zuccotto, ice cream-filled cake
zuchette, zucchini
zuppa, soup
zuppa alla coltivatore, vegetable soup with diced bacon
zuppa alla pavese, soup w/croutons, grated cheese & poached egg
zuppa di arzilla, soup made w/ray fish & broccoli
zuppa di cereali, bean, vegetable & grain stew
zuppa di cipolle alla Francese, french onion soup
zuppa di cozze, mussel soup
zuppa di datteri, fish-soup specialty of Liguria
zuppa di fagioli, bean soup
zuppa di farro, soup made with *farro* (a wheat similar to
    spelt)
zuppa di frutti di mare, seafood soup
zuppa di lenticchie, lentil soup
zuppa di pesce, fish stew
zuppa di pollo, chicken soup
zuppa di telline, soup w/tiny clams
zuppa di verdura, vegetable soup
zuppa di vongole, clam soup w/white wine
zuppa d'orzo, barley & potato soup
zuppa fredda, cold soup
zuppa inglese, not a soup at all. Spongecake soaked in liquor
    w/cream filling & whipped cream
zuppa pavese, clear soup w/a poached egg
zuppa valdostana, cabbage soup from the Val d'Aosta region
zuppa di zucca, soup made from small squash or pumpkin

Zuppa di Farro...
love it.

Buon Appetito.

Phone numbers, days closed and hours of operation often change, so it's advisable to check ahead. Restaurants in tourist areas may have different hours and days of operation during low season. Reservations are recommended for all restaurants unless noted. The telephone country code for Italy is 39.

Prices are for main courses and without wine. Lunch, even at the most expensive restaurants listed below, always has a lower fixed price. Credit cards are accepted unless noted otherwise.

Inexpensive: under 10 euros
Moderate: 11 – 20 euros
Expensive: 21 – 30 euros
Very Expensive: over 30 euros

Amalfi Coast
Da Emilia
This eatery is located in an old boat shed near the Marina Grande in Sorrento. Try to score a table outside so you can watch the fishermen. The emphasis here is on Sorrentine cuisine, like *gnocchi alla Sorrentina* (potato dumplings with a simple tomato-and-cheese sauce). The grilled *calamari* is delicious. This isn't fine dining, but this family-owned place is a nice change from all the fancier restaurants that are prevalent on the Amalfi Coast. *Info*: 62 Via Marina Grande. Amalfi. Tel. 081/8072720. Open daily mar-Nov. www.daemilia.it. Inexpensive – Moderate.

Il Marzialino
This attractive steak house and wine bar is located in the historical center of Sorrento, overlooking the Villa Comunale (the largest public park in Sorrento on a cliff overlooking the Bay of Naples). Featured dishes include *carpaccio con parmigiano e misticanza* (raw Black Angus beef with parmesan and a mixed-green salad) and *lombata di vitello* (veal chop). You won't go home hungry if you order one of the many steaks available. Save room for the delicious *panna cotta* (rich cream custard). They have a very good local wine selection. *Info*: 2 Largo F.S. Gargiulo. Sorrento. Tel. 081/8074406. www.palazzomarziale.com. Moderate – Expensive.

La Caravella

Lovely restaurant in Amalfi known for its celebrity guests and its seafood dishes, especially *calamari* (squid) and *polpo* (octopus). The specialty here is *trito di pesce grigliato in foglia di limone con erba finocchiella e mandorle* (lemon leaves stuffed with finely shredded fish, grilled and served with wild fennel sauce and almonds). The restaurant is known for its extensive wine list, especially those from the Campania region. *Info*: 12 Via Matteo Camera. Amalfi. Tel. 089/871029. Closed Tue and mid-Nov-Jan. www.ristorantelacaravella.it. Expensive – Very Expensive.

Da Gemma

Specialties of Campania (especially seafood), with summer dining on the terrace. Choices include the *zuppa di pesce* (fish stew) for two, *tonno rosso arrostito con broccoli e couscous* (grilled tuna served with broccoli and couscous), and *filetto di manzo con carciofi e patate* (filet of beef with artichokes and potatoes). *Info*: 9 Via Frà Gerardo Sasso. Amalfi. Tel. 089/871345. Closed Wed (Nov to mid-Apr) www.trattoriadagemma.com. Expensive.

Da Aldolfo

After a five-minute boat ride from Positano, you'll arrive at Laurito beach where you'll find this beachfront restaurant and bar. There are changing rooms and showers, and you can rent an umbrella and lounge chair. The specialty here is grilled mozzarella on lemon leaves. Delicious fresh fish dishes, too. Unique! *Info*: 40 Via Laurito. Positano. Accessible by the "red fish" boat departing from the main pier from 10am-1pm and 4pm to about 6:30pm (later on Sat in Jul and Aug). Tel. 089/875022. Closed Oct - Apr. www.daadolfo.com. Moderate.

Cumpa' Cosimo

This family-owned restaurant in Ravello focuses on local dishes. One of the dishes is the simply named *misto*. It's a mix of seven different pastas topped with seven different sauces. Hope you're hungry! You can also order the *frittura di pesce* (fish fry) or meat dishes. *Info*: 44 Via Roma. Ravello. Tel. 089/857156. Closed Mon from Nov-Feb. Moderate.

Assisi

Bibenda

This small, cozy *enoteca* (wine bar) with vaulted ceilings is a must-stop when visiting Assisi. Located on a street off of the Piazza del Comune, you'll be welcomed by sommelier Nila Halun. Wine tastings are offered and feature classic Umbrian wines paired with regional cheeses, homemade bread, *prosciutto* (aged and cured ham), *cinghale* (wild boar), and *cervo* (venison). If you're not interested in a wine tasting, take your pick from the wines by the glass. We enjoyed the "Degustazione Rosso di Assisi," a glass of local red wine paired with *capocollo* (smoked pork salami) for under €10. *Info*: 9 Via Nepis (near Via San Rufino), Tel. 075/8155176. www.bibendaassisi.it. Inexpensive – Moderate.

Medioevo
Located in the historic center of town, you'll dine under stone-vaulted ceilings. Try the excellent *scottadito di agnello* (grilled lamb chop) or the tasty *penne alla norcina* (penne in a sausage-and-cheese sauce). Good selection of Tuscan and Umbrian wines. *Info*: 4B Via dell'Arco dei Priori (near Piazza del Comune). Tel. 075/813068. Closed Sun and Mon. www.ristorantemedioevoassisi. it. Moderate.

Osteria Piazzetta dell'Erba
When the weather is warm, you can sit outside and try the Assisi specialty *torta al testa* (flatbread stuffed with sausage, cheese, and/or vegetables). You can also dine inside under the vaulted brick ceiling surrounded by shelves filled with local wines. For dinner, try the *faraona* (guinea fowl) served in a port sauce with *frutti di bosco* (berries) or the grilled *polipo* (octopus). The wines here are from local vineyards and bottled by the restaurant. *Info*: 15a Via San Gabriele dell'Addolorata (near the Cattedrale di San Rufino). Tel. 075/815352. Closed Mon and mid-Jan to mid-Feb. www.osterialapiazzetta.it. Moderate.

Bologna
Tamburini
This lively place in the city center has been in business since 1932. Locals jam the small eatery to sample pasta dishes. After lunch, it turns into a wine bar. Excellent *affettati misti* (plate of cold cuts and cheese). Great selection of local wines by the glass. Its food shop sells interesting local wine and food specialties. *Info*: 1 Via Caprarie (at Via Calzolerie). Tel. 051/234726. Store open Mon-Sat 8:30am-8pm, Sun 10am-6:30pm. Food served daily noon-6pm. Wine bar opens daily at noon. www.tamburini.com. Inexpensive – Moderate.

Drogheria della Rosa

This friendly *trattoria* with an extensive wine cellar is located in a former pharmacy. The chef presides over this lovely mess of a place. We had the best *lasagne bolognese* here. Don't leave without trying the *tortelli* stuffed with zucchini blossoms. Bologna is the gastronomic capital of Italy, and this place shows you why. *Info*: 10 Via Cartoleria. Tel. 051/222529. Closed some Sun and part of Aug. www.drogheriadellarosa.it. Moderate.

Da Cesari

Romantic restaurant with wood-panelled walls, serving delicious Bolognese dishes. Try the *scaloppa di vitello*. You should try the house specialty, flavorful pork called *mora romagnola*. *Info*: 8 Via de' Carbonesi (south of Piazza Maggiore). Tel. 051/237710. Closed Sun and most of Aug. www.da-cesari.it. Moderate.

Enoteca Italiana

Deli, wine bar, and food-and-wine shop near the famous Neptune Fountain. Great place to stock up on local specialties and snacks for a picnic. They serve great sandwiches, and wine by the glass. *Info*: 2B Via Marsala (north of Piazza Maggiore). Tel. 051/235989. Closed Sun. www.enotecaitaliana.it.

Cremeria Santo Stefano

You'll know when you've arrived at this ice-cream shop, as there is almost always a line to get served. Try the delicious salty pistachio! It's a little outside the city center, but certainly worth the walk. Good choice if you're traveling with children. The shop itself is quite attractive. *Info*: 70/c Via Santo Stefano (at via Remorsella). Tel. 051/227045. Open Tue-Sun 11am-11pm. Closed Mon.

Osteria del Sole

In business since 1465, this fun (and often chaotic) wine bar is a great experience. No food is served here, but you can purchase sausage, ham, bread, and cheese from one of the nearby stores (or at the market) and bring it with you. Enjoy Italian wines by the glass and by the bottle. *Info*: 1/d Vicolo Ranocchi (between Via degli Orefici and Via Pescherie Vecchie). Tel. 348/2256887. Open 11am-9:30pm. Closed Sun. www.osteriadelsole.it. Inexpensive.

Eataly

Eataly is a chain of stores specializing in Italian food and wines. You'll find everything Italian at the Bologna location, including pasta, beer, wine, meats, desserts, and vegetables. You can eat and drink at one of the restaurants, bars, and cafes. There's a *trattoria* on the top floor. We love the attached bookstore. *Info*: 19 Via degli Orafici. Tel. 051/0952820. Open Mon-Thu 9am-11:15pm, Fri and Sat 8am-11:30pm, Sun 10am-11:30pm.www.eataly.it. **FICO Eataly World** bills itself as the world's largest food and agriculture park. It's located about 20 minutes from central Bologna. Open daily 10am-11:00pm. www.eatalyworld.it.

Bologna: Markets
Bologna has two main food markets. Filled with colorful vendors, fresh produce, stinky cheese, and hanging meats, it's really worth the trip to experience the sights and smells.
Mercato di Mezzo: Open daily 9am-11:45pm (Sat until 11pm). Via Peschiere Vecchie near the Piazza Maggiore.
Mercato della Erbe: Open Mon-Thu 7am-midnight, Fri and Sat 7am-2am. Closed Sun. 23 Via Ugo Bassi near the Piazza Maggiore. www.mercatodelleerbe.it.

Bologna: Cooking Classes
The city is known as "Bologna the Fat" for good reason. This is the food city in Italy. What better way to experience the wonderful world of Bologna's cuisine than to attend a cooking school? There are interesting classes offered. Bologna Cooking School offers half day cooking classes where you prepare ragù alla Bolognese. They also offer tours of the sights of the city. For prices and reservations, check out www.bolognacooking-school.com.

Capri
Pulalli
This wine bar and restaurant has a fantastic location next to the clock tower. Not to be missed is the *risotto al limone* (lemon-flavored risotto served in a half lemon). *Info*: 4 Piazza Umberto I. Tel. 081/8374108. Closed Tue and Nov to Easter. Moderate – Expensive.

Le Grottelle
It's worth the hike for the fabulous views from this rustic eatery. Try the *ravioli Capri* (ravioli filled with fresh cheese) or the *pasta con gamberetti e rucola* (pasta with shrimp and arugula). Top off your meal with a glass of *limoncello*. *Info*: 13 Via Arco Naturale. Tel. 081/8375719. Closed Thu (except Jul-Sep) and mid-Nov to Mar. Moderate – Expensive.

Terrazza Brunella

The restaurant at the Villa Brunella Hotel is perfect for a romantic lunch or dinner. The setting is lovely at sunset with a view of the boats in the Marina Piccola. The food is as good as the view. Dishes include *ravioli capresi* (homemade pasta filled with cheese and fresh marjoram) and *salmone al vapore con patate al profumo zafferano* (steamed salmon with potatoes flavored with saffron). *Info*: 24 Via Tragara. Tel. 081/8370122. Open from Easter to the beginning of Nov. www.terrazzabrunella.com. Expensive.

Capri Pasta

On an island as expensive as Capri, this is a great alternative if you're watching your euros. The take-out food is excellent, and its location near the main square is convenient. Choices include *polpettine al vino bianco* (meatballs in a white-wine sauce), *insalata di polpo* (octopus salad), and *ravioli fritti* (fried ravioli). *Info*: 12 Via Parroco Roberto Canale. Tel. 081/8370147. Open daily. Closed Jan and Feb. www.capripasta.com. Inexpensive.

Chianti Wine Route

The Chiantigiana (SR 222) runs from Florence to Siena through vineyards producing Chianti Classico, specifically Chianti Classico DOCG (the highest classification of Chianti). Even if you're not a wine connoisseur, this route is worth the trip. You'll pass beautiful vineyards with ripening Sangiovese grapes and olives, scenic rolling hills, castles, abbeys and churches, and charming Tuscan towns. The trip is especially fun at harvest time (September) when many small towns hold wine festivals. Most of the vineyards along the way are open to the public and have signs inviting you to visit. Look for signs offering *degustazioni* (tastings) and *vendita diretta* (direct sales). Here are just a few towns and wineries that you can visit along the way:

Castello di Verrazzano: They've been producing wine here since the 1100s! You can sample the specialty here (for free), Sassello, made from the Sangiovese grape. *Info*: 32 A Via Citille. Tel. 055/854243. Open daily. www.verrazzano.com.

Greve in Chianti: The small market town of Chianti, big on wine shops, should not be missed. Head to the triangular-shaped Piazza Matteotti for all your wine needs!

Villa Vignamaggio: This villa, just south of Greve, dates back to the 1400s, and the winery produces Chianti Classico, Chianti Classico Riserva, and Vinsanto del Chianti Classico. If you book ahead, you can take part in a guided tour of the gardens and wine cellar, including a wine tasting and lunch. The shop is open daily, and has free wine and olive oil tastings. Oh, by the way, it is here that the woman who posed for da Vinci's "Mona Lisa" was born. *Info*: 5 Via Petriolo. Tel. 055/854661. Shop open daily. www.vignamaggio.com.

Panzano in Chianti: You'll see the castle's tower on the hill as you approach lovely Panzano. You'll have great views of the countryside. The heart of the town is the Piazza Bucci-arelli, where you'll find many shops selling wine and the local embroidery.

Radda in Chianti: This small, attractive village is another center of the wine trade. Stroll the covered walkway that circles the city inside the medieval walls.

Nearby is **Castello di Volpaia**. It's not only a wine estate, but also a small village with accommodations, dining, and (of course) wine shops. You can tour the winery and taste its wines and olive oils in an attractive shop located in the tower. Unique! *Info*: 4 miles north of Radda in Chianti. Tel. 0577/738066. Open daily. www.volpaia.com.

Castellina in Chianti: You won't soon forget Castellina's panoramic views. The town is surrounded by 15th-century walls, and features a 15th-century palace on its main square. You'll also find several restaurants, wine shops, and hotels, making the town a great place to use as your base as you explore the surrounding area.

Cinque Terre
Vernazza Winexperience

This wine bar in Vernazza is a must for wine lovers visiting the Cinque Terre. Not only will you enjoy interesting local wines, but you'll do it while on the patio enjoying an incredible and breathtaking view of the sea. This is the place to be at sunset. You can order a cheese-and-meat platter and other light plates. If you want to taste interesting wines from around Cinque Terre, this is the place to visit. Your host is the charming Alessandro who speaks English and knows his Italian wines. Part of the experience is finding the place. From the main square, walk up the stairs by Gianni Franzi at Via Guidoni, take a left up the steep staircase at Via S. Giovanni Battista, and look for the posters advertising the Winexperience. Ask for help if you get lost! *Info*: 31 Via San Giovanni Battista, Vernazza. Tel. 331/3433801. Open 5pm-9pm. Apr-Oct. www.cinqueterrewinetasting.com. Inexpensive – Moderate.

De Mananan

Hearty fare served in the cellar of a home in the smallest Cinque Terre town. Many dishes feature *pesto*. Try the *pansoti* (triangular-shaped filled pasta). The house specialty is *coniglio* (rabbit) served in a tasty white wine sauce. *Info*: 117 Via Fieschi, Corniglia. Tel. 0187/821166. Closed Mon, Tue, Nov, and part of Jan and Feb. Moderate – Expensive.

Marina Piccola

Dine on delicious *cozze* (mussels) or *zuppe di pesce* (fish stew) at this waterside restaurant. *Info*: 16 Via Lo Scalo, Manarola. Tel. 0187/920923. Closed Mon. www.hotelmarinapiccola.com. Moderate.

Miky

Ligurian seafood, baked in a wood-burning stove, served in this charming Cinque Terre town. Enjoy delicious *antipasti* while you take in the sea view. Do not miss the grilled *calamari*. *Info*: 104 Via Fegina, Monterosso al Mare. Tel. 0187/817608. Closed Tue from Sep to Jul, and all of Nov and Dec. www.ristorantemiky.it. Moderate – Expensive. Just a few doors down at 90 Via Fegina is the more casual **Cantina di Miky**, a popular evening gathering place. Tel. 0187/802525. www.cantinadimiky.it.

Rio Bistrot

Dine on fresh fish and innovative Ligurian cuisine at this bistro above the harbor. Try the *ravioli* or one of the dishes featuring *pesto*. Good local wine selection. *Info*: 10 Via San Giacomo, Riomaggiore. Tel. 0187/920616. Open daily. Moderate – Expensive.

Gambero Rosso

Ligurian specialties at this harborside restaurant (it's been open for over 100 years). The creamy *pesto* is fantastic. End your dinner with a glass of *Sciacchetrà*, a local dessert wine. *Info*: 7 Piazza Marconi, Vernazza. Tel. 0187/812265. Closed Thu and mid-Dec to Mar. www.ristorantegamberorosso.net. Moderate – Expensive.

Belforte

You'll pay for the view at this interesting restaurant located in a medieval tower overlooking the sea. The view won't disappoint and neither will the local specialties served here. Reservations are essential, especially if you want to dine at sunset. Start with the *insalada di polpo* (octopus salad), and you can't go wrong ordering the excellent mixed grill seafood platter. *Info*: 42 Via Guidoni, Vernazza. Tel. 0187/812222. Closed Tue and Nov-Easter. www.ristorantebelforte.it. Very Expensive.

Enoteca Internazionale

This wine bar in Monterosso al Mare is located on the main drag of the *centro storico* (historic center). Sit under one of the umbrellas on the patio and try a local wine from little-known, artisanal producers. The wine bar also features a selection of over 500 wines from all regions of Italy and around the world. You can order snacks to go with your wine (cold cuts, cheese, anchovies, and *bruschetta*). And if you're spending some time in town, you might want to sign up for one of the wine tastings. *Info*: 62 Via Roma, Monterosso al Mare. Tel. 0187/817278. Closed Tue and Jan-Mar. www.enotecainternazionale.com.

Florence   *See Florence maps pages 136 and 137*
Buca Lapi

This restaurant is in a cellar under the Palazzo Antinori. Try the *scampi giganti alla griglia* (large grilled shrimp) under the vaulted ceiling, surrounded by old travel posters. The Florentine specialty *bistecca alla fiorentina* served here is a large, grilled T-bone steak, served rare. You might want to start your dinner with a bowl of *ribollita* (which means "reboiled"), a famous Tuscan soup made with bread and vegetables. There are many variations but the main ingredients always include leftover bread, beans, and vegetables such as carrots and cabbage. *Info*: 1r Via del Trebbio (at Via dei Tornabuoni). Tel. 055/213768. Closed Sun and part of Aug. No lunch. www.bucalapi.com. Expensive.

Casa del Vino

This small, friendly, and attractive wine bar serves cheese, sausage, ham, cured meat, and sandwiches. Good selection of wines by the glass, especially wines from Tuscany. The staff will also help you pick out a bottle to drink in your hotel room or to take home. *Info*: 16/r Via dell'Ariento (off of Via Sant'Antonino). Tel. 055/215609. Closed Sat (in Jun, Jul, and Sep), Sun and part of Aug. www.casadelvino.it. Inexpensive.

Il Cibrèo and Cibreino

Florentine cuisine at this famous, attractive, and popular restaurant and *trattoria*. Try the *sformato* (souffle). This is the place to sample the traditional Tuscan specialty of *trippa* (tripe). The lively *trattoria* (Cibreino) shares a kitchen with the restaurant and is less expensive (note that the *trattoria* does not take reservations). *Info*: Restaurant: 8r Via Verrocchio (off of Via de' Macci), Trattoria: 122r Via de' Macci, Caffè: 5r Via Verrocchio. Tel. 055/2341100 (restaurant). www.cibreo.com. Moderate (*trattoria*) – Expensive (restaurant).

Coquinarius

This intimate, casual restaurant is located on a small street near the Duomo. A wide selection of reasonably priced salads and entrees make it a great choice for lunch. Try the pear and pecorino ravioli. They are known for their *carpaccio* (thinly sliced raw beef). You can also order wild boar, salmon, and octopus *carpaccio*. Lots of tourists. *Info*: 11/r Via dell'Oche (at Via della Studio). Tel. 055/2302153. Open daily. No lunch Mon-Fri. www.coquinarius.com. Moderate.

Enoteca Pitti Gola e Cantina

This warm and friendly *enoteca* (wine bar) is located opposite the Pitti Palace. A great choice for lunch or dinner when in the Oltrarno (the neighborhood south of the Arno River). It's just a short walk from the Ponte Vecchio. You need to book in advance, especially for dinner, since there are only six tables. Two brothers and a friend run the place, where the emphasis is on wines from Tuscany. They have an excellent selection of wines from Chianti. You can choose fresh pasta dishes, local cheese, and *salumi*. They also have wine tastings and a wine-tasting lunch. *Info*: 16 Piazza Pitti. Tel. 055/212704. Open noon to 11pm. Closed Tue. www.pittigolaecantina.com. Moderate.

Frescobaldi Wine Bar

Small, attractive wine bar and restaurant with excellent pasta dishes and a wide selection of wines by the glass. Try the *piatto di gran salumi Toscani* (assorted Tuscan salamis). Main dishes include *carrè di agnello* (rack of lamb) and *involtini di vitella ripiena di zucchine e prosciutto* (veal roll stuffed with zucchini and cured ham). The Frescobaldis have owned a vine-

yard for over 700 years. *Info*: 2-4r Via dei Magazzini (between
Piazza della Signoria and Via d. Condotta). Tel. 055/284724.
Open daily. www.frescobaldifirenze.it. Moderate – Expensive.

Mario
This eatery near San Lorenzo and the Mercato Centrale has
been in business for over sixty years. Simple traditional
Florentine dishes are served at communal tables. Start with
zuppa di fagioli (bean soup), and for your main course try
peposo di manzo (beef stew), *tagliata di manzo al rosmarino*
(boneless beefsteak with rosemary), or the tasty *bistecca
di maiale* (pork chop). *Info*: 2R Via Rosina (at the Piazza
Mercato Centrale). Tel. 055/218550. Open noon-3:30pm.
Closed Sun and Aug. No reservations. www.trattoriamario.com.
Inexpensive – Moderate.

Trattoria La Casalinga
This unassuming *trattoria* is located near the church of Santo
Spirito south of the River Arno. The name means "house-
wife," and you'll find Tuscan specialties here. Tables are
quite close together, where you'll dine with a mixture of tourists and locals. It's known for its *ribollita* (vegetable soup
thickened with bread) and for its decent pasta dishes such as
pasta Bolognese. Try the *coniglio al forno* (baked rabbit) for
something different. *Info*: 9/r Via Michelozzi. Tel. 055/218624.
Closed Sun and part of Aug. www.trattorialacasalinga.it.
Moderate.

Trattoria Le Mossacce
Dine with locals and tourists on Florentine cuisine at reasonable prices. The restaurant has been around since the early
1900s. Florentine favorites such as *ossobuco* (braised veal
shank), *trippa* (tripe), and *ribollita* (vegetable soup thickened
with bread) are featured here. This is not fine dining. Dishes
are simple, and the house wine is a decent Chianti. *Info*: 55r
Via del Proconsolo (near Piazza del Duomo). Tel. 055/294361.
Closed Sat, Sun and Aug. No reservations. www.trattorialemos-
sacce.it. Inexpensive – Moderate.

Le Volpi e l'Uva
This *enoteca* (wine bar) is located south of the Arno River
between the Ponte Vecchio and the Pitti Palace. There's a

109

good selection of the Italian and French wines from lesser-known wineries. You can also munch on an equally good selection of Italian and French cheese, cured meats, and *crostini*. *Info*: Piazza de'Rossi (off of Piazza Santa Felicita). Tel. 555/2398132. Open Mon-Sun 11am-9pm. Closed Sun. www.levolpieluva.com. Inexpensive – Moderate.

Florence: Gelato and Food Shops

Florence claims to be the birthplace of *gelato* (ice cream). That may or may not be true, but everyone in the city seems to have an opinion on the best place to have it. Here are a few suggestions.

Carapina: This *gelateria* (ice-cream shop) is known for its fruit flavors. Try the interesting sweet and salty gorgonzola. *Info*: 2 Piazza Oberdan. Tel. 055/676930. www.carapina.it.

Il Procopio: Known for its unusual combination of flavors, the specialty here is "La Follia:" a *gelato* with caramelized figs, toasted almonds, and *Sachertorte* (the Austrian chocolate cake). Delicious! *Info*: 60R Via Pietrapiana (at Via dei Pepi). Tel. 555/2346014. Closed Mon.

Vivoli: This Florentine institution serves up some delicious flavors, everything from *fico* (fig) to *limoncini alla crema* (vanilla with lemon peels). *Info*: 7R Via Isola delle Stinche (a block west of Via G. Verdi, a backstreet near Piazza di Santa Croce). Tel. 055/292334. Closed Mon. No credit cards. www.vivoli.it.

Vestri: Chocolate, chocolate, and more chocolate. Especially good is the chocolate *gelato*. The attractively wrapped chocolates, in pale blue containers, make great souvenirs. *Info*: 11/r Borgo Albizi (at Piazza G. Salvemini). Tel. 055/2340374. No credit cards. www.vestri.it. Closed Sun.

Florence: Food Market
Mercato Centrale

The ground floor of the huge Central Market is loaded with meat, fish and cheese. Upstairs you'll find fresh produce, wine, and homemade pasta. A great place to stock up for a picnic! There's a modern food court upstairs with plenty of places to eat. *Info*: Piazzale del Mercato Centrale (between Via Nazionale and Via Sant' Antonino). Open daily 8am-midnight. www.mercatocentrale.com.

Milan

Boeuc

Milan's oldest restaurant in an elegant setting near the Duomo. The *scalloppina con funghi porcini* (veal scallop in a porcini mushroom sauce) is fantastic. Known for its impeccabe service. *Info*: 2 Piazza Belgioioso. Tel. 02/76020224. Closed Sat, Sun (lunch) and Aug. Metro: Duomo. www. boeucc.it. Expensive – Very Expensive.

Bar Martini/Martini Bistrot

Milan is synonymous with fashion. So it's not surprising that designers Dolce & Gabbana have opened this bar, lounge, and restaurant near one of their boutiques. Very trendy and very fashionable. More of a Milan design experience than a dining experience, although the food can be quite good – and the people-watching is excellent. *Info*: 15 Corso Venezia. Tel. 02/76011154. Open daily. Metro: San Babila. www.dolcegabbana.com/martini. Expensive.

Cavallini

Dine indoors or outside under the covered patio at this restaurant near the central train station. Try the *cotoletta alla milanese* (breaded veal cutlet) or *ravioli alla "Cavallini"* (homemade ravioli with meat sauce and cream). *Info*: 2 Via Mauro Macchi (at Via Napo Torriani). Tel. 02/6693174. Closed Sat (lunch) and Sun. Metro: Centrale. www.anticaosteriacavallini.it. Moderate – Expensive.

Luini

You'll find this lunch-time favorite just one block from the cathedral and near the east entrance to the Galleria Vittorio Emanuele II. Here you'll find be the Milanese specialty *panzerotto*. Similar to a *calzone* or an *empanada*, the dough is slightly sweet and deep-fried, which gives them a crispy exterior. You can choose any number of ingredients, but most order the classic version with tomato sauce and mozzarella. This is food-on-the-go (there is nowhere to sit). A great idea if you're watching your euros, as they cost about €3. A popular choice is *cipolle, olive, e pomodoro* (onion, olives, and tomato). You can also order one baked like *mozzarella, pomodoro, acciughe, e olive nere* (mozzarella, tomato, anchovy, and black olives). There are also sweet versions, including *ricotta e rioccolato* (ricotta cheese and chocolate). *Info*: 16 Via Santa Radegonda. Tel. 02/86461917. Open Mon 10am-3pm, Tue-Sat 10am-8pm. Closed Sun. www.luini.it. Metro: Duomo. Inexpensive.

Nerino Dieci

Great value at this attractive *trattoria* with a courteous staff. Try one of the many grilled dishes, including *pesce spada* (swordfish), *costolette di agnello* (lamb cutlet), or *gamberoni* (large prawns). *Info*: 10 Via Nerino (off of Via Torino). Tel. 02/39831019. Closed Sat (lunch) and Sun. Metro: Duomo. www.nerinodieci.it. Moderate.

Al Pizzetta

This small, inexpensive, and comfortable *pizzeria* will not disappoint. Most of the small pizzas offered cost €3. Favorites include the *funghi* (mushroom), *salsiccia* (sausage), and *tonno e pomodori* (tuna and tomato sauce). Wash it down with a large glass of beer. *Info*: 73 Viale Monte Nero (near Piazza Cinque Giornate). Tel. 02/36508599. No lunch Sat and Sun. Metro: Porta Romana. www.alpizzetta.it. Inexpensive.

Il Salumaio di Montenapoleone

This is an interesting spot for lunch. There's a deli, cafe, and restaurant. The setting is the star attraction, as it's located in the neo-Renaissance courtyard of the Bagatti Valsecchi Museum. The neighborhood is filled with boutiques, so it's a good place to relax after shopping. Generous, homemade pasta dishes are the specialty here. Don't miss the *burrata*, a very buttery cheese from Apulia, the creamy *risotto milanese*, or the *pasta arrabbiata* (pasta with a spicy tomato and herb sauce). Interesting wine selection featuring the wines of Lombardy. *Info*: 10 via S. Spirito/5 via Gesù. Tel 02/76001123. Closed Sun. Metro: Montenapoleone. www.ilsalumaiodimontenapoleone.it. Metro: Montenapoleone. Expensive.

Milan: Pastry

Paticceria Marchesi: Marchesi has been serving pastries since 1824. Have a delicious cup of coffee with your treats. You must try the *cannoncini* (cream-filled puff pastry horns). *Info*: 11 via S. Maria alla Porta (off of via Meravigli). Tel. 02/862770. Open Mon-Sat 7:30am-8pm, Sun 8:30am-1pm. Closed Mon. Metro: Cordusio. www.pasticceriamarchesi.it.

Milan: Café

Camparino: A café has been at the corner of the Piazza del Duomo and the Galleria Vittorio Emanuele II since 1867. It has a fantastic Belle Epoque interior, but the real attraction here is the great people-watching. You should order a *campari* (the bitter, red Italian aperitif made with a blend of herbs and spices). *Info*: Galleria Vittorio Emanuele II. Tel. 02/86464435. Open daily. Metro: Duomo.www.camparino.it.

Milan: Food Stores
Peck

Founded in 1883, this temple to gourmet eating and drinking includes a bakery, prepared foods, deli, butcher shop, and renowned wine cellar. There's a restaurant upstairs that serves traditional Milanese dishes. *Info*: 9 Via Spadari (at Via Victor Hugo). Tel.02/8023161. Shop closed Mon morning, Restaurant closed Mon. Metro: Duomo. www.peck.it.

Eataly Milano Smeraldo

Eataly is a chain of stores specializing in Italian food and wines. You'll find everything Italian, including pasta, beer, wine, meats, desserts, and vegetables. You can also eat and drink at one of the restaurants, bars, and cafes in this large space, and you can even take a cooking class! *Info*: 10 Piazza XXV Aprile. Tel. 02/49497301. Open daily 8:30am to midnight. Metro: Porta Garibaldi. www.eataly.net.

Naples
Antico Forno delle Sfogliatelle Calde Fratelli Attanasio

Just a few blocks from the central train station, this old bakery is the place to have *sfogliatelle*, meaning many leaves or layers. These crisp, layered pastries resemble seashells when baked, and are filled with sweetened *ricotta*, semolina, cinnamon, and candied orange or lemon zest. When you arrive, take a number first and then get ready to taste this delicious traditional Neapolitan pastry. *Info*: 1-4 Vico Ferrovia . Tel. 081/285675. Open 6:30am to 7:30pm. Closed Mon. www.sfogliatelleattanasio.it. Inexpensive.

Brandi

Many places claim to have made the first pizza, but it's likely that the first *pizza margherita* (tomato, mozzarella, and basil) was made here. They also serve pasta dishes. So what if it's touristy? *Info*: 2 Salita Santa Anna di Palazzo (off of

Via Chiaia). Tel. 081/416928. Open daily. www.brandi.it.
Inexpensive – Moderate.

Da Michele

This *pizzeria* (open since 1870) was featured in the Julia
Roberts film "Eat, Pray, Love." You'll need to get a number and
likely wait for a while. There are only two offerings here: *pizza
marinara* (tomato, oregano, and garlic) and *pizza margherita*
(tomato, mozzarella, and basil). *Info*: 1 Via Sersale (off of Corso
Umberto between Piazza N. Amore and Piazza Garibaldi). Tel.
081/5539204. No credit cards. Closed Sun and part of Aug.
www.damichele.net. Inexpensive.

L'Ebbrezza di Noe

This is an *enoteca* (wine bar) during the day and a restaurant for
dinner. You'll sit in small rooms surrounded by bottles of wine
on shelves. The staff is friendly and attentive, and will guide you
through ordering one of the many wines from the Campania region
that are available here. The menu changes frequently (there's no
written menu, only a blackboard menu). The *antipasti* features a
mixture of six meats, cheeses, a quail egg, toast, and eggplant. The
specialty here is *carpaccio di chianina* (thinly sliced raw Tuscan
steak). A real find and an excellent place to experience wine from
small local producers. *Info*: 8-9 Vicolo Vetriera a Chiaia. Tel.
081/400104. Closed Mon and Sun (dinner). www.lebbrezzadinoe.
com. Moderate.

Tandem

This homey, no-frills *trattoria* specializes in *ragu*. There are two
choices: vegetarian and meat. You can choose pasta as a base,
or just dip thick pieces of bread into the sauce. The menu also
features staples such as meatballs and pork dishes, but most come
here for the *ragu*. You can purchase the house wines (including a
surprisingly good sparkling *rosso*) by the carafe or glass. *Info*: 51
Via G. Paladino (off of Piazzetta Nilo). Tel: 081/19002468. Open
daily. www.tandem.napoli.it. Inexpensive.

Palazzo Petrucci

This elegant restaurant with minimalist décor, located in a
villa overlooking the Gulf of Naples, serves innovative dishes.
For your starter try the delicious *zuppa di castagne* (chestnut
soup) that includes beans and *pancetta* (cured pork belly).
Main courses include *agnello con albicocche, pecorino e*

114

menta (lamb served with apricots, pecorino cheese, and mint). They also have a five-course tasting menu for €90. The restaurant has an extensive wine list. *Info*: 16/c Via Posillipo. Tel. 081/5757538.Reservations required. www.palazzopetrucciristorante.it. Very Expensive.

Orvieto
Le Grotte del Funaro
Umbrian specialties served in a *grotte* (cave). Windows provide a sweeping view of the countryside below. Try the *ravioli con brasato di chianina* (ravioli with braised beef). The specialty here is *grigliata mista* (a plate of grilled meats including sausage, lamb, and pork). *Info*: 41 Via Ripa Serancia. Tel. 0763/343276. Closed Mon and part of Jul. www.grottedelfunaro.it. Moderate.

Enoteca Al Duomo
This *enoteca* (wine bar) and wine shop is located on Piazza Duomo. You can sip your wine while you view the facade of the town's fantastic Gothic cathedral. In addition to cheese and meat plates, you can order pasta dishes and *panini* (sandwiches). This is the place in Orvieto to have a glass of *Orvieto Classico*, the delicious local wine made from Trebbiano grapes. *Info*: 13 Piazza Duomo. Tel. 393/6901083. Closed some Thu, www.enotecaduomo.com. Inexpensive – Moderate.

Palermo
Antica Focacceria San Francesco
Stuffed *focaccia* sandwiches and Sicilian snacks at this 1834 bakery in the heart of Old Town. Delicious *arancini* (deep-fried rice balls). A Palermo institution! *Info*: 58 Via Paternostro. Tel. 091/320264. Open daily. www.afsf.it. Inexpensive.

Ottava Nota
Innovative Sicilian dishes are served at this modern restaurant in the Kalsa district. Start with the *tartare di tonno e avocado* (tuna tartar and avocado). Other dishes include the tasty *risotto con asparagi e gambero* (risotto with asparagus and shrimp) and *petto d'anatra all'arancia* (duck breast with orange). Attentive service and a wine list featuring lesser-known Sicilian wines. *Info*: 55 Via Butera. Tel. 091/6168601. Closed Sun. No lunch. www.ristoranteottavanota.it. Expensive.

Casa del Brodo

This restaurant near the Vucciria Market (see below) has been in business since the late 1800s. If you're interested in no-nonsense Sicilian dishes, come here to try *macco di fave* (meatballs and tripe) or *fritella di fave* (fried fava beans). The house specialty is the hearty *tortellini in brodo* (homemade pasta in a beef broth). *Info*: 175 Corso Vittorio Emanuele. Tel. 091/321655. Closed Tue. www.casadelbrodo.it. Moderate.

Vucciria

In the heart of the *centro storico*, this market is filled with colorful vendors, fresh produce, stinky cheese, and hanging meats. It's really worth the trip to experience the sights and smells. Not to be missed are the stands selling olives, artichokes, and flavorful blood oranges. *Info*: The streets around the Piazza San Domenico. Closed Sun.

Ballarò

It's said that a food market has been on this site for 1000 years. You'll find vendors selling vegetables, cheeses, spices, meat, and fresh fish. There are plenty of stands for you to have a snack. Seek out the stands selling *panelle* (slices of dough made from chickpeas that are deep-fried with slices of eggplant). Also popular here is the Palermo specialty of *pane ca' meusa* (calf's-spleen topped with cheese). *Info*: The streets around Piazza Carmine (between Via Marqueda and Corso Tukory). In the Albergheria district.

Antico Caffè Spinnato

Dating back to 1860, this is Palermo's oldest café. Sicilians are known for their sweets, and you can sample scrumptious cakes, cocktails, coffee, and *gelati* here. *Info*: 115 Via Principe di Belmonte (off of Via Ruggero Settimo). Tel. 091/583231. www.spinnato.it.

Pisa
Il Bistrot

This friendly, intimate restaurant and wine bar is located between the train station and the Leaning Tower. Start with the delicious *bruschetta*. For your first course, order *pasta Pici* (pasta with cheese, pears, and black pepper) and try the *filetto di maialino* (pork tenderloin) in a gorgonzola sauce. Order a bottle of wine from a local vineyard. A real find. *Info*: 17 Piazza Chiara Gambacorti. Tel. 349/0759809. Closed Wed. No lunch on Sat or Sun. www.ilovebistrot.it. Moderate.

La Sosta dei Cavalieri

This intimate and friendly restaurant is a great choice for lunch or dinner. It's a short walk from the Leaning Tower. Try the delicious *tagliolini al sugo di piccione* (thin noodles with a pigeon sauce) or the *cannelloni alla erbe di campo e pinoli* (cannelloni with wild herbs and pine nuts). *Info*: 3 Via San Frediano (off of Piazza dei Cavalieri). Tel. 050/9912410. Closed Sun and part of Aug. www.sostadeicavalieri.it Moderate.

Vicolo Divino

This attractive wine bar with a stone floor and outdoor seating in warm weather is located near the River Arno. The staff is welcoming, and the local wine selection is excellent. You'll be offered (free) snacks from the small buffet at the bar, or you can order a cheese-and-meat platter. *Info*: 10 Filippo Serafini (off of Lungarno Pacinotti). Tel. 377/9428446. Closed Sun and most of Aug. No lunch Thu and Sat. www.vicolodivino.it.
Inexpensive – Moderate.

Rome   *See Rome maps pages 138-144*
L'Angolo Divino

Taste and buy wines from every region of Italy at this pleasant wine bar near the Camp de'Fiori. Have a light lunch or dinner, as they serve salads, cured meats, and cheese. *Info*: 12 Via dei Balestrari (near the Campo de' Fiori). Tel. 06/6864413. Closed Mon (lunch), Sun (lunch), and part of Aug. www.angolodivino. it. Inexpensive – Moderate. Map C, #1.

Antica Roma

This unique *hostaria* is built into ancient ruins about three miles outside central Rome (about a 20-minute taxi ride). Always a warm welcome. You'll dine on Roman and Mediterranean specialties. Try the *mazzancolle al vino blanc* (large prawns in a white-wine sauce), *salmone con le mandorle* (salmon in an almond-and-cream sauce), or *scaloppini al marsala* (thin slices of veal in a Marsala-wine sauce). An experience. *Info*: 87 Via Appia Antica. Tel. 06/5132888. Closed Mon and Sun (dinner). Moderate – Expensive.

Antico Arco

Attentive service, a modern setting, and fine Roman food make this a popular place. Excellent *carrè di agnello* (rack of lamb). Delicious chocolate desserts. It's a little out of the way at the top of Janiculum Hill. The wine list has 1200 selections from Italy and all over the world. You can order a bottle of *La Tache Romanée Conti 2009* for €1,800 (we opted for the house *Chianti*). *Info*: 7 Piazzale Aurelio. Tel. 06/5815274. Open daily. www.anticoarco.it. Moderate – Expensive. Map C, #2.

Babette

Inspired by the film "Babette's Feast," your feast should include the *filetto di manzo alla griglia* (grilled beef filet served with a basil sauce). Great buffet lunch. Start with the *zuppa di verdure con pesto* (vegetable soup seasoned with a light basil pesto). The wine list features over 100 selections from Italy and France. Opt for the *Casale del Giglio Chardonnay* from Lazio (the area around Rome). There's a charming courtyard where you can dine in summer. *Info*: 1D-3 Via Margutta. Tel. 06/3211559. Closed Mon and part of Aug. www.babetteristorante.it. Moderate – Expensive. Map A, #3.

Il Bacaro

Small, unpretentious restaurant on a small alley near the Piazza delle Copelle (a huge ivy covers the entrance). You are welcomed with a complimentary glass of *prosecco* and a small appetizer. Delicious *risotto* dishes, and try the *involtini di pesce spada con gamberi* (swordfish roulades with shrimp) or *ventaglio di tonno con pomodori secchi e riduzione di aceto balsamico* (tuna with sun-dried tomatoes and balsamic vinegar). *Info*: 27 Via degli Spagnoli. Tel. 06/6872554. Open daily. www.ilbacaroroma.com. Moderate-Expensive. Map B, #4.

Osteria del Cavaliere

This small, unpretentious, family-owned restaurant serves Italian fare with an emphasis on dishes from the Abruzzo region. You'll receive a warm welcome and dine with mostly locals. Try the *chicche di patate ai 5 formaggi* (small potato gnocchi with five cheeses) or the *tagliata di manzo alla griglia* (sliced grilled beef). Don't be put off by its somewhat out-of-the-way location. *Info*: 32 Via Alba (between Via Appia Nuova and Via Tuscolana). Tel. 06/64850434. Closed Sun. No lunch. Moderate. Map E, #5.

Centro

It's often difficult to find good places to eat near a main train station. This restaurant is near the Termini train station and is an exception to that rule. The hamburger "Centro" is a popular choice. It's served with cheddar cheese and a barbeque sauce. For more Italian fare, try the *spaghetti cacio e pepe* (spaghetti served with a sauce made of black pepper and pecorino cheese). The rich *fondant al cioccolato* is served with an orange sauce. Very friendly service. *Info*: 61 Via Cavour. Tel. 06/48913935. Open daily for breakfast, lunch, and dinner. www.ristorantecentro.it. Moderate. Map D, #6.

Cavour 313

A huge wine list and selection of cured meats and cheeses make this a good place for a light meal. The pork tenderloin crusted with pistachio nuts is delicious. *Info*: 313 Via Cavour (near the Forum and Colosseum). Tel. 06/6785496. Closed part of Aug. www.cavour313.it. Inexpensive – Moderate. Map E, #7.

Cul de Sac

Wines from throughout the world are offered at this wine bar near Piazza Navona. Nice selection of wines by the glass. A plus is the outdoor seating that stays open until a bit past midnight. The interesting menu features everything from duck ravioli to roast beef in an "esterhazy" sauce (with mushrooms, sour cream, and paprika). You can also order salads and sweets here. Great people-watching. The wine list resembles a telephone book, and features over 1500 selections. *Info*: 73 Piazza Pasquino. Tel. 06/68801094. Open daily. www.enotecaculdesa-croma.it. Moderate – Expensive. Map B, #8.

Dar Poeta

Choose thick- or thin-crust pizza at this popular and inexpensive eatery in the Trastevere neighborhood. If you have room, try the *calzone* with Nutella (chocolate-hazelnut spread) and *ricotta* cheese. *Info*: 45 Vicolo del Bologna (off of Via della Scala). Tel. 06/5880516. Open daily. www.darpoeta.com. Inexpensive – Moderate. Map C, #9.

Enoteca Corsi

Wine bar serving Roman cuisine at common-seating tables in a 1937 storefront. An economical choice for lunch. Try the white lasagna with artichokes. Be advised that this restaurant is in many guidebooks and can often be filled with tourists. *Info*: 87/88 Via del Gesú (off of Via del Plebescito). Tel. 06/6790821. Open Mon-Sat lunch, Wed-Fri dinner. Closed Sun and Aug. www.enotecacorsi.com. Inexpensive. Map B, #10.

'Gusto

You'll find something for every food lover at this complex located on and around the Piazza Augusto Imperatore. A *ristorante* (restaurant), *pizzeria*, and grill are at #9 on the piazza. The restaurant serves hearty traditional Roman fare. Try the delicious *pasta cacio e pepe* (pasta with pecorino, parmesan cheese and black pepper). There's a glass-enclosed *formaggeria* (cheese shop) featuring cheeses from throughout Italy. *Info*: 9 Piazza Augusto Imperatore (near Via del Corso). Tel. 06/3226275. Open daily. www.gusto.it. Moderate – Expensive. Map A, #11.

Il Convivio Troiani

Elegant and acclaimed restaurant. It's formal with what can be described as old-fashioned décor. The food is excellent, but whatever you have, make sure you start your dinner with the memorable *fiori di zucca in pastella con mozzarella* (fried zucchini flowers filled with mozzarella cheese). The excellent *coniglio e nocciole* (rabbit with hazelnuts) is a featured dish. The tasting menu (six courses) is €125. *Info*: 31 Vicolo dei Soldati (between Piazza Navona and Piazza Umberto I). Tel. 06/6869432. Closed Sun and part of Aug. No lunch. www.ilconviviotroiani.com. Expensive – Very Expensive. Map B, #12.

Mizio's Street Food

Delicious large sandwiches, pizza, and vegetarian options at this small shop not too far from the Colosseum. There's also a selection of beer and wine. No seating here, so try to get a seat around the fountain at the nearby Piazza della Madonna dei Monte. *Info*: 55 Via degli Zingari. Tel. 06/64008396. Open Mon-Wed 9am-9:30pm, Thu-Sat 9am-1:30am. Closed Sun. www.miziostreetfood.it. Inexpensive. Map E, #13.

Pizza E Mozzarella

This tiny eatery, with just a few tables, is not much to look at from the outside. It's known for its delicious traditional pizza.

Good choice of toppings. You can down your slice with an Italian *birra* (beer)! Some argue that it's the best pizza in Rome. *Info*: 32 Via del Pie' di Marmo (between Via del Gesù and Via della Gatta). Tel. 3273579195. Open 11am-9pm. Closed Sun. Inexpensive. Map B #14.

Polese

Enjoy outdoor and indoor dining at this *trattoria* on the charming Piazza Sforza Cesarini. Try the *fettuccine alla Polese* (fettuccine w/cream and mushrooms). *Info*: 40 Piazza Sforza Cesarini (off of Corso Vittorio Emanuele not too far from Piazza Navona). Tel. 06/6861709. Closed Tue. www.trattoriapolese.com. Moderate. Map B, #15.

Another *trattoria* on the same piazza at #24 is **Da Luigi**. Try the delicious *penne alla vodka*. Tel. 06/6865946. Closed Mon. www.trattoriadaluigi.com. Moderate. Map B, #15.

Roscioli

A little bit of everything at this deli, wine bar, and restaurant. At the deli you can choose from 300 types of cheese, 150 varieties of cold cuts, nearly 3,000 wine bottles, and a large selection of Italian food specialties. The restaurant, **Ristorante Salumeria Roscioli**, offers a huge selection of cheeses, meats, pastas, and main courses like the simple and delicious *cacio e pepe* (pasta with a sauce made of black pepper and pecorino cheese). *Info*: 21/22 Via dei Giubbonari. Tel. 06/6875287. Deli open Mon-Sat 8:30am-8:30pm. Restaurant open Mon-Sat 12:30pm-midnight. Both closed on Sunday. Roscioli also has wine tastings and cooking classes. Reserve at www.salumeriaroscioli.com. Map C, #16.

Nearby, you can visit the bakery **Antico Forno Roscioli** and coffee shop **Roscioli Caffè**. *Info*: Bakery: 34 Via dei Chiavari. Tel. 06/6864045. Open Mon-Sat 7am-7:30, Sun 8am-6pm. www.anticofornoroscioli.it. Coffee shop: 16 Piazza Benedetto Cairoli. Tel 06/89165330. Open Mon-Sat 7am-11pm, Sun 8am-6pm. Closed part of Aug. www.rosciolicaffe.com.

La Terrazza dell'Eden

This very expensive and formal restaurant (jacket and tie required) in the Hotel Eden (several blocks off the Via Veneto)

offers memorable food and an unforgettable view of St. Peter's.
It's known for its veal tartare starter and its braised *Chianina*
beef. *Info*: 49 Via Ludovisi. Tel. 06/47812752. Closed Tue.
www.dorchestercollection.com. Very Expensive. Map A, #17.

Vini e Buffet

This unpretentious Roman eatery with friendly staff is off the
Campo Marzio and Via del Corso. The entrance to the small
restaurant is covered with vines. You'll sit at wooden tables
where you can order sandwiches, vegetarian dishes, salads,
soups, or pasta. At lunch, workers from the nearby Parliament
drop in, and in the evening the place is quieter and less
crowded. There's also a decent selection of wine by the glass or
bottle. *Info*: 60 Vicolo della Torretta. Tel. 06/6871445. Closed
Sun. Moderate. Map A, #18.

Al Vino Al Vino

The name of this tiny and unpretentious *enoteca* (wine bar)
means "wine to wine." Several wines by the glass are offered
daily. There's a selection of meats and cheeses. The specialty
here is *caponata* (eggplant and capers in a sweet and sour
sauce). Join the locals watching football (soccer). Relaxing,
unassuming, and comfortable. The Colosseum is just down the
street. *Info*: 19 Via dei Serpenti. Tel. 06/485803. Open daily
10am-2pm and 6pm-midnight. Metro: Cavour. Inexpensive-
Moderate. Map D, #19.

Vinoteca Novecento

This small wine bar has a good selection of wine, *prosecco*, and
grappa. This is a great place to have a cheese-and-salami plate
or a plate of meatballs while trying wine from all regions of
Italy. You can sit outside on tables made of wine barrels in good
weather, or inside surrounded by walls decorated with wine
crates and jammed with wine bottles. *Info*: 47 Piazza Delle
Coppelle (near Piazza Navona). Tel. 06/6833078. Open daily.
Moderate. Map B, #20.

Enoteca Ferrara

This interesting place in the Trastevere neighborhood provides
plenty of options for wining and dining. Housed in a building dating back to the 1400s, you can see the large wine cellar through an ancient grate. We like to enjoy a glass of wine

and appetizers at "La Mescita," the wine bar. If you want to dine, you have two options: Ferrarino's Tavern is an *osteria* where you can have the house *gnocchi* served with either clams or Spanish ham. The more formal and expensive name-sake restaurant serves innovative dishes featuring everything from *faraona* (guinea fowl) to *baccalà* (cod). *Info*: 41 Piazza Trilussa. Tel. 06/58333920. Open daily. www.enotecaferrara.it. Moderate (*osteria*) – Expensive (restaurant). Map C, #21.

Rome: Food and Wine Stores

Buccone: This wine bar is a great place for lunch, and you can also buy wines from every region of Italy. *Info*: 19 Via di Ripetta (near the Piazza del Popolo). Tel. 06/3612154. Closed Sun. www.enotecabuccone.com. Map A, #22.

Castroni: A food market offering specialties from every region of Italy (and other countries). Huge pasta selection. Try a cup of delicious Italian coffee. *Info*: 196 Via Cola di Rienzo (near San Pietro). Tel. 06/6874383. Open daily. www.castronico-ladirienzo.it. Shops also at 79 Via Frattina. Tel. 06/69921903 and 102 Viale G. Marconi. Tel. 06/5574272. Map F, #23.

Eataly: Roam through 170,000 square feet crammed with Italian food and specialties. There are 18 restaurants and cafes, a brewery, coffee shops, and food and wine shops. A must for every foodie. *Info*: 1492 Via Piazzale XII Ottobre (in the Air Terminal next to Stazione Ostiense). Piramide metro (Line B). Take the underpass to Stazione Ostiense. Five-minute walk to the Air Terminal. Tel. 06/90279201. Open daily 9am to mid-night (individual shops and restaurants have different hours of operation). www.roma.eataly.it.

Moriondo e Gariglio: Many of the 80 delicacies that are for sale at this historic chocolate shop (established in 1850) are made with the same 19th-century recipes. Don't miss the dark-chocolate truffles! *Info*: 21 Via Piè di Marmo (near Piazza del Collegio Romano). Tel. 06/6990856. Closed Sun. Map B, #24.

Trimani: 180-year-old store with over 5,000 wines, liqueurs and grappas. *Info*: 20 Via Goito (near Stazione Termini). Tel. 06/4469661. Closed Sun. www.trimani.com. Map D, #25. The Trimani Wine Bar is around the corner at 37/b Via Cernaia (Closed Sun). Tel. 06/4469630.

123

VyTA: Enoteca Regionale del Lazio: Wine bar and restaurant featuring regional culinary products and wine. Delicious antipasti, especially the *carciofi alla romana* (artichokes stuffed with garlic, parsley and mint, cooked in olive oil and white wine). They also sponsor wine tastings featuring the wines of the Lazio region. *Info*: 94 Via Frattina (near the Spanish Steps). Tel. 87716018. Open daily. Map A, #26.

Rome: Coffee
Tazza d'Oro: This coffee shop near the Pantheon is a great place to taste great Italian coffee (*caffè*). On a hot day in Rome, try a *granita de caffè* (coffee served over crushed ice) and on a chilly day, get a thick, rich, and decadent hot chocolate (*cioccolata calda*). Go to the cash register to order and then take your receipt to the counter. *Info*: 84 Via degli Orfani. Tel. 06/6789792. Open daily. www.tazzadorocoffeeshop.com. Map B, #27.

Antico Caffè Greco: This historic and elegant café opened in 1760 and is Rome's oldest. It's located on one of Rome's most exclusive shopping streets leading to the Spanish Steps. Formal waiters will serve you as they did former regulars such as Casanova, Keats, and Byron. You'll pay for the lavish surroundings as a *cappuccino* costs €12 (less if you stand at the bar with the locals). Cocktails begin at €20. *Info*: 86 Via dei Condotti. Tel. 06/6791700. Open daily. www.anticocaffegreco. eu. Map A, #28.

Rome: *Gelato*
Giolitti: Everyone seems to have an opinion on the best place to have *gelato*. So, head to this shop near the Pantheon like others have for over a century. It's especially known for its variety of fruit flavors. *Info*: 40 Via degli Uffici del Vicario (next to the Camera dei Deputati della Repubblica Italiana). Tel. 06/6991243. Open daily 7am to 1:30am. www.giolitti.it. Map B, #29.

Gelateria dei Gracchi: Get in line for some of the best *gelato* in all of Italy. This shop, a short walk from the Vatican, uses all-natural ingredients. Known for its delicious pistachio. We loved the dark chocolate! *Info*: 272 Via dei Gracchi. Tel. 06/3216668. Open daily. Map F, #30.

Sweet Life: This popular *gelato* shop is located on the main street Corso Vittoria Emanuele II. Quite a few vegan choices are available. It's known for its *stracciatella*, vanilla ice cream with bits of chocolate. *Info*: 270 Corso Vittorio Emanuele II. Tel. 3206336587. Open daily. Map B, #31.

Rome: Food Markets
Campo de' Fiori: Via del Giubbonari. Mon-Sun 7am-3pm. A food market has been held here since the 1800s. Even if you're not food shopping, head to this attractive square to get a glimpse of Roman life.

Nuovo Mercato di Testaccio: Via Benjamin Franklin (between Via Luigi Galvani and Via Aldo Manuzio). Mon-Sat 6am-3pm. The Testaccio Market has moved to a new, modern building. Filled with colorful vendors, stinky cheese, fresh produce, poultry, and meat. www.mercatotestaccio.com.

Nuovo Mercato Trionfale: Via Andrea Doria (near the Cipro Metro stop). Mon-Sat 7am-2pm (until 5pm on Tue and Fri). There are 250 vendors at this crowded and popular market.

Rome: Cooking Classes and Wine Tastings
Enoteca Corsi (above) sponsors cooking classes held in a medieval castle in Rome. Your host, Dario, is an expert on Italian art. He'll guide you around the castle and discuss its works of art. Claudia is a sommelier who will walk you through the process of shopping at Rome's food markets for the fresh ingredients used in traditional Roman dishes. Classes and lunch are held in the apartments of Pope Paolo V and Pope Leo XII. This one-day class is a unique cooking-and-art seminar. *Info*: Reservations can be made through the Enoteca Corsi website www.enotecacorsi.com or through www.3inchfat.com. There are several other tours and classes available. Prices start at €180.

Eat and Walk Italy: Make pasta, pizza, and other Italian favorites at these cooking classes. All classes take place at locations within walking distance of Rome's main sights (St. Peter's, Pantheon, Trevi Fountain, and the Spanish Steps). Several classes available starting at €40. *Info*: Tel. 39085086. www.eatandwalkitaly.it.

In Rome Cooking: Cooking classes and food tours include pizza and *gelato* making, pasta making, full meals, and kids and family classes. *Info*: Tel. 06/68805375. www.inromecooking.com. Classes starting at €70. The company also operates **Passetto Restaurant** at 41 Piazza di S. Apollinare. Tel. 06/62286019. www.ristorantepassetto.it.

Vino Roma: This wine studio (in a sleek, modern space with a thousand-year-old cellar) is located in the heart of Rome near the Colosseum. Friendly English-speaking hosts guide you through wine tastings. The motto here is "We love drinking wine, but not being snobbish about it." The most popular tasting is "My Italians" where you will taste six Italian wines from different wine regions of Italy (€50). Other options include wine and cheese tastings (€60), wine and dinner (price varies), and food tours. *Info*: 84/G Via in Selci (off of Via Giovanni Lanza). Be careful about the address as 84/G is seven doors down from 84 Via in Selci! Tel. 3284874497. Metro: Cavour. Reservations only at www.vinoroma.com.

Old Frascati Wine Tour: *Frascati* is one of the most famous Italian wines. It's produced in an ancient town in the hills just south-east of Rome. The charming town of Frascati is only a 25-minute train ride from Rome. This popular wine tasting and day trip includes a tour of the vineyard and 16th-century farmhouse. Sip you wine while enjoying the fabulous views of Rome in the distance. *Info*: Tel. 3283898372. Wine tastings begin at €55 and can be booked through www.oldfrascati.com.

San Gimignano
Bel Soggiorno
Tuscan specialties served in a 100-year-old hotel located in this beautiful walled town. For your first course, have the *pappardelle di pasta fresca al sugo di cinghiale* (fresh pappardelle pasta in wild-boar sauce). For a main course, the *costolette d'agnello* (lamp chop) is delicious. Lots of game dishes on the menu. Fantastic views of the countryside from the terrace. *Info*: 91 Via San Giovanni (in the Hotel Bel Soggiorno). Tel. 0577/943149. Closed Wed, part of Nov, Dec, part of Feb, and part of Mar. www.ristorante-belsoggiorno. it. Moderate – Expensive.

Enoteca di Vinorum

San Gimignano is crowded with day trippers, so if you want or need a break from the crowds (especially in high season), this wine bar is a good choice. Housed in former stables, if you score a table outside (there are only a few tables) you'll be rewarded with a scenic view. Good selection of *antipasti* (cheese, meats, *bruschetta*, salads) and an excellent selection of wine by the glass. This is the place to try *Vernaccia di San Gimignano*, a local dry white wine with a slight peppery taste. *Info*: 30 Piazza della Cisterna/21 Via degli Innocenti. Tel. 0577/907192. Open daily. Closed Jan to mid-Mar. www.divinorumwinebar.com. Moderate.

Dorandò

This small and elegant restaurant is housed in a 14th-century building in the center of town. You'll dine on Tuscan specialties such as *controfiletto al Chianti Classico* (sirloin in a Chianti wine sauce) under vaulted ceilings. Large selection of Tuscan wines. *Info*: 2 Vicolo dell'Oro (between Piazza Cisterna and Piazza Duomo). Tel. 0577/941862. Closed Mon. Open daily from Easter to Nov. www.ristorantedorando.it. Expensive.

Enoteca Gustavo

San Gimignano can be quite expensive, so visiting a wine bar for a simple snack and drink can be a way to save money. This casual wine bar is another great place to try local wines, especially *Vernaccia di San Gimignano*, the popular local dry white wine. There's a sign in the window boasting "World's Best Bruschetta." That may be an exaggeration, but the *bruschetta* with melted *pecorino* cheese certainly is great with your wine. Other light meals are available. *Info*: 29 Via San Matteo. Tel. 0577/940057. Open daily. Inexpensive – Moderate.

Siena

Le Logge

Tuscan dishes at this *osteria* near the Piazza del Campo (one of Italy's most beautiful squares). In the 19th century, this was a simple grocery store. Today, it's a wonderful place to dine, especially if you can score a table outside. Try the *cinghiale* (wild boar). The house specialty is *malfatti all'osteria* (spinach-and-ricotta dumplings in a cream sauce). *Info*: 33 Via del Porrione (a street off of Piazza del Campo). Tel. 0577/48013. Closed Sun and part of Jan. www.osterialelogge.it. Moderate – Expensive.

Osteria La Sosta di Violante

Sosta means "break," and this *osteria* is a perfect place to take a break from the crowds. Just a short walk from the Piazza del Campo, you'll find this friendly eatery filled with locals and a few tourists. This isn't fine dining, but there's rustic local fare such as *pici cacio e pepe* (eggless pasta with a sauce of pecorino cheese and black pepper) and *risotto al Chianti* (*risotto* in a Chianti wine sauce). *Info*: 115 Via Di Pantaneto. Tel. 0577/43774. Closed Sun. www.lasostadiviolante.it. Moderate.

Tuscan Wine School

If you have a few hours and want to learn about Italian and Tuscan wines, head here. Classes are taught in English. Two-hour classes with six wines are €45. *Info*: 26 Via Stalloreggi (near Piazza de Conte). Tel. 333/5707011. Closed Sun. www.tuscanwineschool. com (on-line reservations).

Turin
Al Bicerin

Founded in 1763, this tiny café is a great place to stop when visiting the market at the nearby Piazza della Repubblica (Mon to Sat 8am-2pm). Order a *bicerin*, a combination of chocolate, coffee, and cream. *Info*: 5 Piazza della Consolata. Tel. 011/4369325. Open 8:30am-7:30pm. Closed Wed and Aug. www.bicerin.it. Moderate.

Da Cianci Piola Caffé

Piedmontese food at reasonable prices at this friendly *trattoria*. When choosing something from the chalkboard menu, try a delicious *coniglio* (rabbit) dish. Tables spill out onto the charming square in good weather. *Info*: 9B Largo IV Marzo. Tel. 011/19879451. Open daily. Inexpensive.

Angolo 16

Foodies will love this modern restaurant with an open kitchen. The restaurant is part of the "Slow Food" movement (which emphasizes locally grown products and regional cuisine). The menu features dishes from the Liguria and Piedmont regions of Italy and all the ingredients are from local farmers and breeders. The wine list focuses on lesser-known wines from the Piedmont region. *Info*: 16 Via San Dalmazzo. Tel. 011/2478470. Closed Sun (dinner) and Mon. www.angolo16.com. Moderate –Expensive.

Baratti e Milano

This historic café dates back to 1858 and is famous for its chocolates, especially *gianduiotti* (hazelnut chocolates). You'll feel like you stepped back in time while you indulge in the pastries, ice cream, coffee, and drinks here. It's located in the glass-covered Galleria Subalpina. *Info*: 29 Piazza Castello. Tel. 011/4407138. Closed Mon. www.barattiemilano.it.

Eataly Torino Lingotto

The Turin location of this large food emporium is located in a former factory building. The "Slow Food" movement (which emphasizes locally grown products and regional cuisine) began in the area, and there's a large section devoted to the movement. You'll find cheese, meats, homemade pasta, sauces, and pastries. Wines from Piedmont are also featured here, so it's a great place to try Barbera, Nebbiolo, and Moscato. *Info*: 230 Via Nizza (From central Turin, take the metro to Lingotto stop). Tel. 011/19506801. Open daily 10am-10.30pm. www.eataly.net.

Venice   *See Venice maps pages 146-152*
Santa Croce/San Polo neighborhoods

Antico Giardinetto

Friendly, informal, family-run osteria. Try the *filetto di manzo ai 3 pepi* (filet of beef with pepper sauce) or *costolette d'agnello Toscano scottadito* (Tuscan roasted lamb chops). There are many seafood options on the menu, including *soutè di cozze e vongole* (sautéed mussels and clams). Decent house red wine, too. *Info*: 2253 Santa Croce, Calle dei Morti (near Campo San Cassiano). Rialto vaporetto. Tel. 041/722882. www.anticogiardinetto.it. Closed Mon and part of Jan. No lunch. Moderate – Expensive. Map B #1.

Il Refolo

This *pizzeria*/restaurant is on a picturesque square overlooking the church of San Giacomo dell'Orio. Customers dock their boats along the patio for take-out. Try the pizza topped with a local specialty, *castraure* (the first floral shoot of the artichoke). One pizza on the menu features roasted figs and *proscuitto*. *Info*: 1459 Santa Croce. Campiello del Piovan (Campo San Giacomo dell'Orio). Riva di Biasio or San Stae vaporetto. Tel. 041/5240016. Closed Mon and Dec-Mar. Moderate. Map B #2.

La Bottiglia

Dining in Venice can be expensive, but that doesn't mean that you have to spend a lot of money to have good food. This simple eatery is near the Basilica di Santa Maria Gloriosa dei Frari. Choose your meat and cheese and create a *panini* (sandwich) on *focaccia* (flat oven-baked bread similar to pizza dough). There's no indoor seating, but a few tables outside are near the canal. Good local wine and beer. *Info*: 2537 San Polo. Campo San Stin. San Toma vaporetto. Tel. 3355930910. Open daily. Inexpensive. Map: B #3.

Al Bacco Felice

Just a ten-minute walk from Piazzale Roma, this neighborhood restaurant and *pizzeria* is popular with both locals and tourists. Nothing fancy here. Pizza, pasta and traditional Italian dishes like pasta *arrabbiata* (pasta with a spicy tomato and herb sauce). Complimentary Venetian cookies are served at the end of your meal. *Info*: 197/e Santa Croce on Corte dei Amai. Piazzale Roma vaporetto. Tel. 041/5287794. Open daily. Moderate. Map B #4.

San Marco neighborhood
Da Ivo

Beautiful restaurant serving Venetian (and Tuscan) specialties. Try the delicious *bistecca alla Fiorentina* (T-bone steak). We came here before celebrities like George Clooney came here. So, he's just copying us. *Info*: 1809 San Marco. Calle dei Fuseri (near Campo S. Luca). Tel. 041/5285004. www.ristorantedaivo.it. Closed Sun and Jan. San Marco vaporetto. Expensive – Very Expensive. Map D #5.

Enoteca al Volto

This wine bar has wooden tables and chairs, wine labels as wallpaper, an impressive wine list, and simple Venetian fare. Try the *ravioloni di asparagi con capesante e fiori di zucca* (asparagus ravioli with scallops and zucchini flowers). A good deal. *Info*: 4081 San Marco. Calle Cavalli (near Campo Chiesa and Campo San Luca). Rialto vaporetto. Tel. 041/5228945. www.enotecaalvolto.com. Open daily. Moderate. Map D #6.

Da Mamo

Pasta, pizza, and large salads at this cozy and casual *trattoria*.

Good value. Try the *pizza diavola* with tomato, mozzarella, and spicy salami. Although it's a bit corny, they have a *pizze zodiaco* menu featuring a pizza named after the twelve signs of the zodiac. *Pizza Toro* (Taurus) is topped with tomato, mozzarella, sausage, brie, and pepperoni. *Info*: 5251 San Marco. Calle Stagneri (near Campo San Bartolomio). Rialto vaporetto. Tel. 041/5236583. www.damamo.it. Open daily. Moderate. Map D #7.

Vino Vino
Popular wine bar and restaurant (near the Teatro La Fenice) serving typical Venetian cuisine and offering 200 Italian and imported wines by the bottle or glass. Try the local specialty, *sarde in saor* (sardines in a sweet-and-sour sauce). *Info*: 2007A San Marco. Ponte delle Veste (between La Fenice and via XXII Marzo). Tel. 041/2417688. www.vinovinowine.com. Open daily. Vaporetto: S. Maria del Giglio. Moderate. Map D #8.

Castello neighborhood
Dal Moro's - Fresh Pasta To Go
This unassuming and hard to find take-out place is hugely popular. Pasta is made fresh on the premises, and you can order any number of sauces. The *arrabbiata* (spicy tomato and herb sauce) is particularly good. A great way to save money in Venice, where dining can be quite expensive. Each serving costs around €7. Despite the crowds, the servers are very friendly. *Info*: 5324 Castello. Calle de la Casseleria (near the church of Santa Maria Formoso). Rialto or San Marcovaporetto. Tel. 041/4762876. www.dalmorosfreshpastato-go.com. Open daily. No credit cards. Closed Sun. Inexpensive. Map D #9.

Al Mascaron
You might have to sit next to strangers (mostly tourists) at long tables in this unpretentious restaurant/bar. The food is straightforward Venetian. Try the deep-fried *calamari*. The specialty here is *spaghetti allo scoglio* (spaghetti with lobster, shrimp, and scallops). *Info*: 5225 Castello. Calle Lunga Santa Maria Formosa (near the Campo Santa Maria Formosa). Rialto vaporetto. Tel. 041/5225995. www.osteriamascaron.it. Closed Sun and Jan. No credit cards. Moderate. Map D #10.

Oliva Nera

Expect a warm welcome at this small, charming *osteria*. Try the *ossobuco* (braised veal shank), *baccalà* (salt cod), or dishes served with *nero di seppia* (black squid ink). You might even leave with a complimentary bottle of the house olive oil. *Info*: 3417/3447 Castello. From Riva degli Schiavoni (on the water-front), turn onto Calle della Pietà, left on Calle Bosello to Salizada dei Greci. San Zaccaria vaporetto. Tel. 041/5222170. www.olivanera.com. Closed Wed. Moderate – Expensive. Map E #11.

Al Covo

Fresh Venetian specialties (especially seafood) at this small *osteria*. Try the *fritto misto* (mixed deep-fried fish). *Info*: 3968 Castello. Campiello della Pescaria (off of Riva degli Schiavoni). Arsenale vaporetto. Tel. 041/5223812. www.ris-torantealcovo.com. Closed Wed and Thu. Expensive. Map E #12.

Cannaregio neighborhood

Malibran

Intimate restaurant, complete with Venetian-glass chandeliers, near the Rialto Bridge. The interesting *pizza della casa* has tomatoes, mozzarella, ham, mushrooms, salami, artichokes, and an egg on top. Pasta dishes include *tortellini panna, proscuitto, e funghi* (tortellini pasta with cream, ham, and mushrooms). Gluten-free choices are available. *Info*: 5864 Cannaregio. Off of Salizzada San Giovanni Grisostomo and overlooking the Teatro Malibran. Rialto vaporetto. Tel. 041/5228028. www.hotelmalibran.com. Open daily. Moderate. Map D #13.

Vini da Gigio

Wine bar and *osteria* serving Venetian specialties and home-made pasta. Delicious *gnocchi*. There are two seatings on Sat and Sun (7pm and 9pm). *Info*: 3628A Cannaregio. Fondamenta San Felice (just off the Strada Nuova). Cá d'Oro vaporetto. Tel. 041/5285140. www.vinidagigio.com. Closed Mon, Tue, part of Jan and part of Aug. Moderate – Expensive. Map A #14.

Osteria al Cicheto

This small *bacaro* (small, local bar) is near the Santa Lucia train station. If you just want to sample *ciccheti*, head to the bar. You'll have a choice of at least ten wines by the glass, most from the Veneto region. If you want to dine, make reservations as there are only a few tables. You'll dine on Venetian specialties such as *fegato alla veneziana con i fichi* (liver with figs) and *pasta e fagioli all veneta* (Venetian pasta and beans). You'll have an interesting experience! *Info*: 367/A Cannaregio. Calle della Misericordia. Ferrovia vaporetto. Tel. 041/716037. Closed Sat (lunch) and Sun. www.osteria-al-cicheto.it. Moderate. Map A #15.

Dorsoduro neighborhood
Ai Gondolieri
Not for seafood lovers. This restaurant serves meat dishes like *ossobuco di vitello* (braised veal shank). Try the creamy *risotto con funghi porcini* (risotto with porcini mushrooms). Delicious *fiori di zucca* (zucchini flowers filled w/cheese, then battered and fried). *Info*: 366 Dorsoduro. Calle S. Domenico Dorsoduro. Fondamenta dell'Ospedaleto (near the Guggenheim Museum at Fondamenta Venier dai Leoni). Accademia vaporetto. Tel. 041/5286396. www.aigondolieri.it. Open daily. Moderate – Expensive. Map C #16.

La Bitta
In a small storefront, this family-owned restaurant and wine bar focuses on meat dishes (often accompanied by grilled vegetables). The *porchetta* (roast suckling pig stuffed with herbs), served with a horseradish sauce, is delicious. The menu also features dishes served with *peverada* (a spicy sauce with chicken livers and anchovies). Desserts include an excellent *panna cotta* (rich cream custard). Wine comes in a bottle, but you only pay for what you've consumed. End your meal with *grappa*. *Info*: 2753A Dorsoduro. Calle Lunga San Barnaba (off of Campo San Barnaba). Ca' Rezzonico vaporetto. Tel. 041/5230531. Closed Sun and part of Jul. No lunch. No credit cards. Moderate. Map C #17.

Cantine del Vino già Schiavi
You'll find a decent selection of Italian wine by the bottle at this wine shop. Head to the bar (there's no seating here) where you can sample *cicchetti* for around €2. Try the interesting specialty *tartare di tonno*, tuna dusted with unsweetened cocoa powder. There's a large selection of wine by the glass, most

from the Veneto region, starting at €2. If you ask for a *fuori*, you'll be served your wine in a plastic cup so that you can take it outside. *Info*: 992 Dorsoduro.(near the Accademia Museum on the San Trovaso canal). Zattere or Accademia vaporetto. Tel. 041/5230034. Open 8:30am-10:30pm. Closed Sun. www.cantinaschiavi.com. Inexpensive. Map: C #18.

Estro

This wine bar and restaurant is decorated with wood furnishings and Murano glass. The vast wine list features more than 600 wines mostly from Italy and France. If you dine here, start with the house specialty *baccalà mantecato* (creamed cod) and don't miss the rich lasagna with veal ragout and *parmigiano reggiano*. *Info*: 3778 Dorsoduro. Calle San Pantalon. San Toma vaporetto. www.estrovenezia.com. Tel. 041/4764914. Closed Tue. Map B #19.

Venice: Food Markets
Rialto Market (Rialto vaporetto). Produce Market: Mon-Sat 7:30am-1pm. Fish Market at Campo de la Pescheria: Tue-Sat 7:30am-1pm.
Garibaldi Market on via Giuseppe Garibaldi (Arsenale vaporetto). Mon-Fri 8am-noon.

Drinking in Venice
Caffè Florian
Piazza San Marco (St. Mark's Square) is home to this elegant and expensive café. It has been in business since 1720, and it's worth the splurge to sit and listen to the orchestra in one of the world's loveliest squares. In fact, you'll pay more when the orchestra performs. When the weather isn't great, you can sit inside surrounded by mirrors, statues, and frescoes. Expect to pay at least €20 for a *Bellini* (prosecco and peach nectar). *Info*: 56 Piazza San Marco. San Marco vaporetto. Tel. 041/5205641. Closed Wed in winter. Open daily 9am-midnight. www.caffe-florian.com. Map D #20.

Al Prosecco
You can't come to Italy and not sample *prosecco*. This sparkling white wine will tickle your tongue and quench your thirst, especially on a warm Venetian night. Great terrace and simple *cichetti* (the Venetian version of Spanish tapas). A glass of

prosecco begins at €4 and goes up from there. *Info*: 1503 Santa Croce. Campo San Giacomo de l'Orio. San Stae vaporetto. Tel. 041/5240222. Closed Sun, Aug, and Jan. www.alprosecco.com. Map B #21.

Harry's Bar
Travelers continue to flock to Harry's Bar just west of St. Mark's Square. Although dinner is extremely expensive (and many complain not worth the cost), most come to have a martini or delicious *Bellini* (sparkling prosecco and peach nectar) at the bar. The drink will cost you around €20, so drink it slowly! If it was good enough for Ernest Hemingway and Truman Capote, it should be good enough for you. *Info*: 1323 Calle Vallaresso. San Marco vaporetto. Tel 041/5285777. Open daily. www.cipriani.com. Map D #22.

Venice: Ciccheti Bars
Ciccheti, the Venetian version of tapas, are served at bàcari (small, local bars) with glasses of wine. Starting at as little as €1, you'll pay a fraction of the cost that you would at a café. It's a great way to eat on a budget. Here are a few places to try ciccheti. (All are near the Rialto vaporetto)
Cantina do Mori: 429 San Polo. Calle do Mori and Calle Miani (on the San Polo side of Rialto Bridge, walk to end of the market stalls, turn left and then immediately right). Tel. 041/5225401. Closed Sun. Try the *melanzane alla parmigiana* (eggplant parmesan). Map F #A.
Bancogiro: 122 San Polo. Campo San Giacometto (west end of Rialto Bridge along the Grand Canal). Tel. 041/5232061. Closed Mon. www.osteriabancogiro.it. Try the *selezione di formaggi* (cheese plate). Map F #B.
Al Mercà: 213 San Polo. Campo Cesare Battisti. On a picturesque square in Rialto Markets area (off of Fondamenta Riva Olio). Tel. 347/1002583. www.osteriaalmerca.it. Try the *robiola* (soft, mild, and slightly sweet cheese). Map F #C.
Cantina Do Spade: 859 San Polo. 19 Calle Do Spade, On a narrow alleyway near Campo Beccarie. Tel. 041/5210583. www.cantinadospade.com. No lunch Tue. Try the *calamari fritti* (fried squid). Map F #D.
All'Arco: 436 San Polo. Calle Arco. Calle de l'Ochialer. Tel. 041/5205666. Closed Sun. Try the *acciughe* (anchovies). Map F #E.

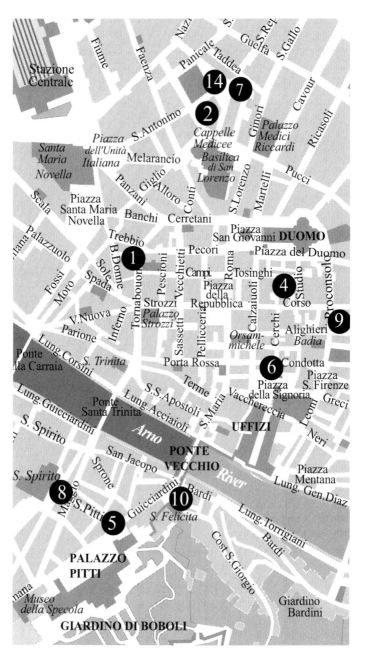

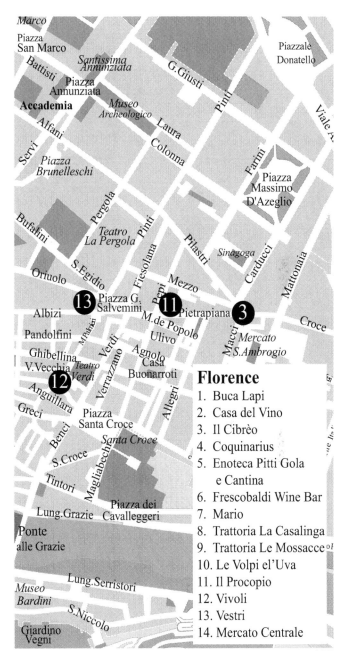

Florence

1. Buca Lapi
2. Casa del Vino
3. Il Cibrèo
4. Coquinarius
5. Enoteca Pitti Gola
   e Cantina
6. Frescobaldi Wine Bar
7. Mario
8. Trattoria La Casalinga
9. Trattoria Le Mossacce
10. Le Volpi el'Uva
11. Il Procopio
12. Vivoli
13. Vestri
14. Mercato Centrale

Tuscany and Umbria

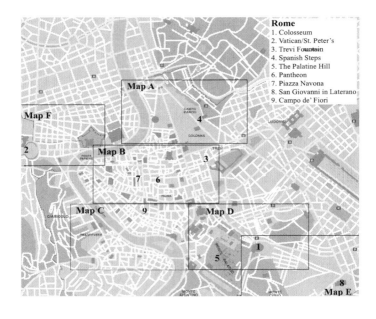

Rome
1. Colosseum
2. Vatican/St. Peter's
3. Trevi Fountain
4. Spanish Steps
5. The Palatine Hill
6. Pantheon
7. Piazza Navona
8. San Giovanni in Laterano
9. Campo de' Fiori

Rome Map A - Spanish Steps

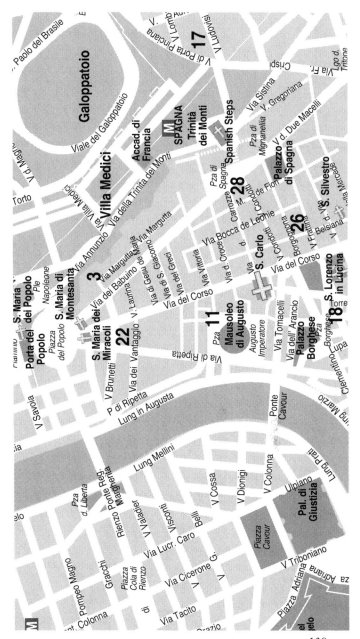

Rome Map B - Piazza Navona/Pantheon/
Trevi Fountain

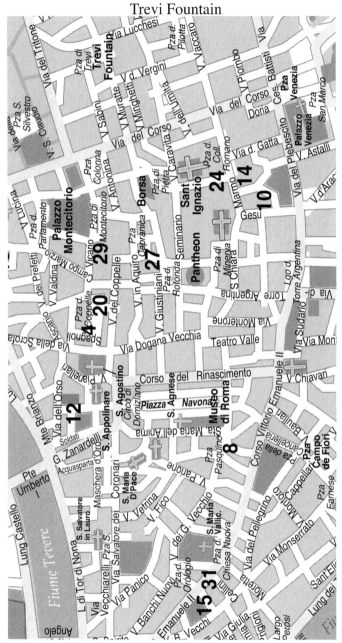

Rome Map C - Campo de' Fiori/Trastevere

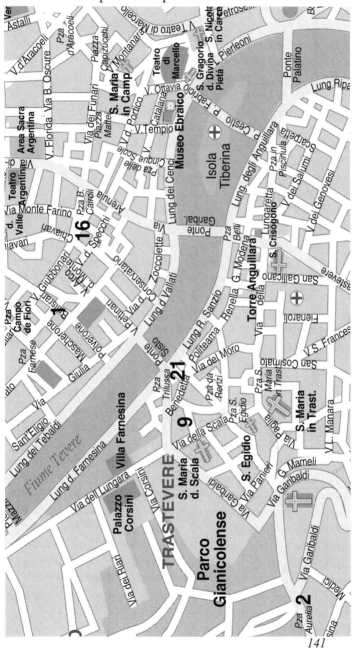

Rome Map D - Termini/Colosseum

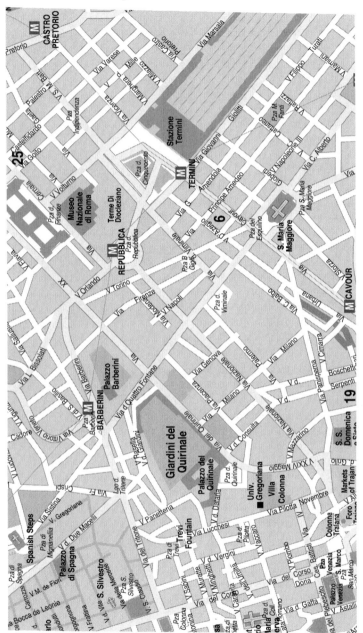

Rome Map E - Colosseum/San Giovanni in Laterno

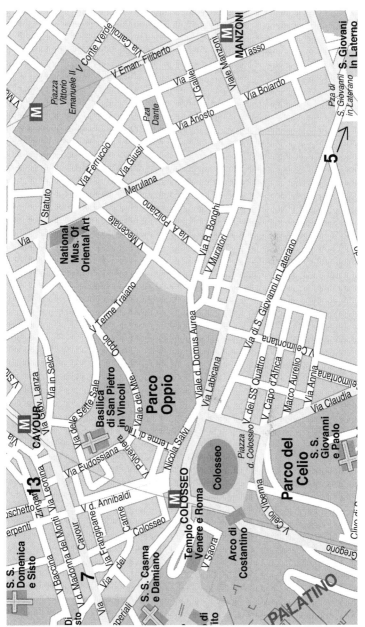

Rome Map F - Vatican

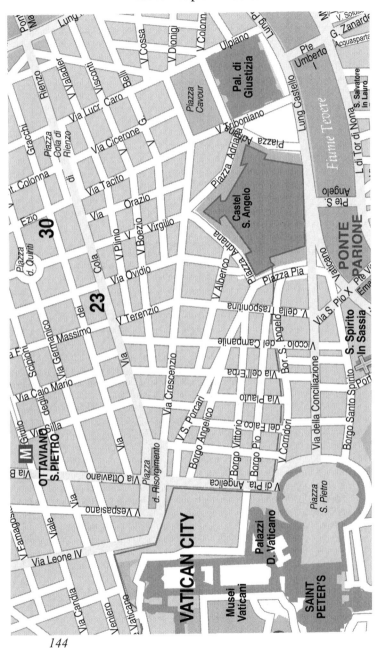

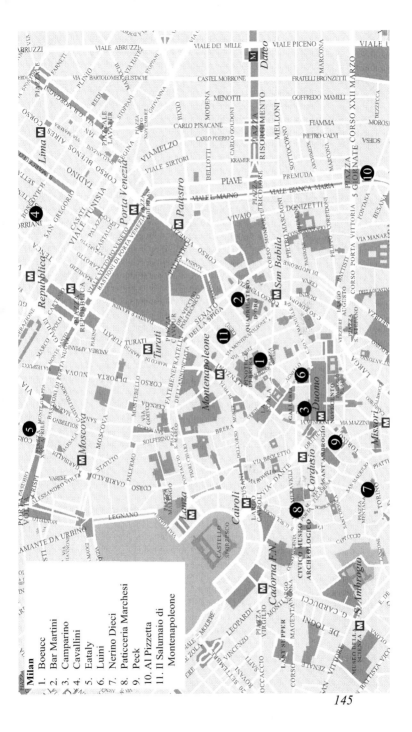

Milan

1. Boeucc
2. Bar Martini
3. Camparino
4. Cavallini
5. Eataly
6. Luini
7. Nerino Dieci
8. Paticceria Marchesi
9. Peck
10. Al Pizzetta
11. Il Salumaio di Montenapoleone

145

Venice Overview

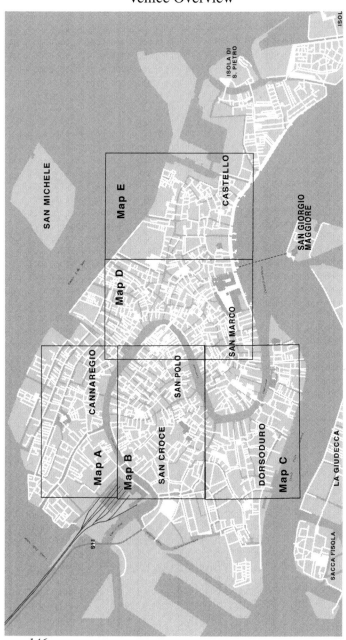

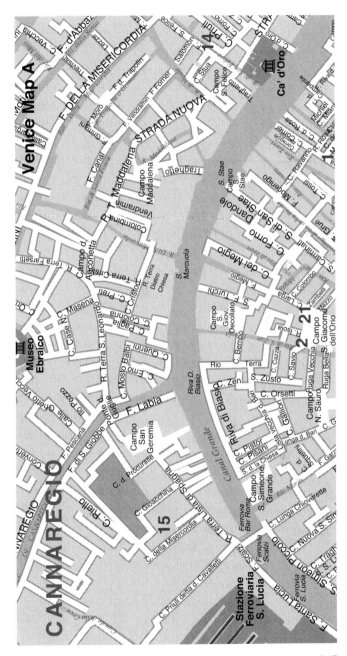

Venice Map A

CANNAREGIO

STRADA NUOVA

Ca' d'Oro

Museo Ebraico

Stazione Ferroviaria S. Lucia

14

15

2 21

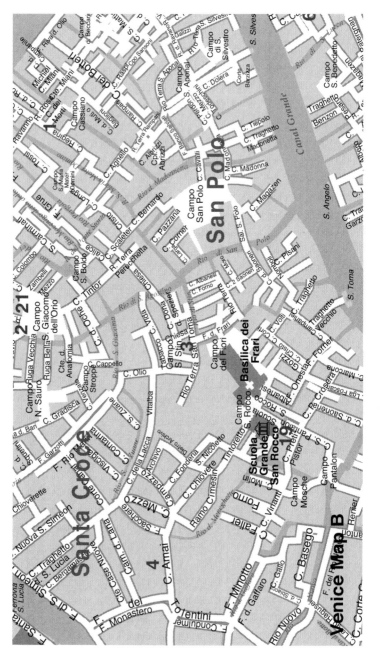

Venice Map C

S. Marco

Dorsoduro

Gallerie Academia

Guggenheim

Ponte Academia

Canal Grande

Campo Santa Margherita

Campo Carmini

Corte Contarini

C. Raguseo

S. Maria Del Giglio

F. Salute

Campo S. Maurizio

Campo S. Maria Zobenigo

Campo Pisani

Campo Francesco Morosini

Campo S. Vidal

Ca' Rezzonico

Campo S. Samuele

Campo S. Stefano

Campo S. Barnaba

Campo S. Agnese

Campo S. Trovaso

Zattere

Canale Della Giudecca

Salute

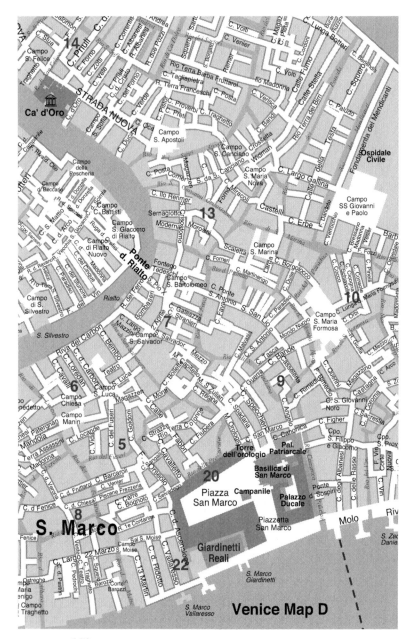

Venice Map D

150

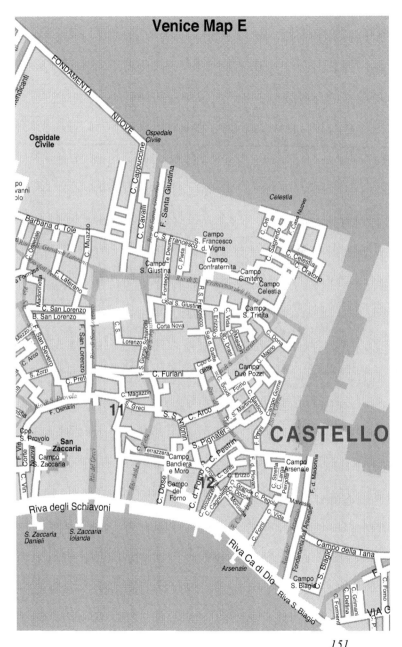

Venice Map E

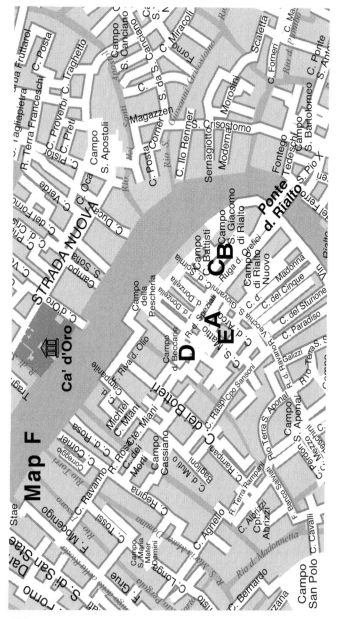

Map F

Ca' d'Oro

Ponte d. Rialto

STRADA NUOVA

Campo S. Apostoli

Campo della Pescheria

Campo di Beccarie

del Botteri

Campo S. Giacomo di Rialto

Ruga d. Orefici

Campo Rialto Nuovo

Campo Cassiano

C. Regina

Campo S. Maria Mater Domini

Campo San Polo

Restaurants by Location
Descriptions of restaurants in the cities listed here can be found on the page number following each city.

Europe Made Easy Travel Guides

Eating & Drinking Guides
Menu Translators and Restaurant Guides

- *Eating & Drinking in Paris*
- *Eating & Drinking in Italy*
- *Eating & Drinking in Spain and Portugal*
- *Eating & Drinking in Latin America*

Europe Made Easy Travel Guides

- *Amsterdam Made Easy*
- *Barcelona Made Easy*
- *Berlin Made Easy*
- *Europe Made Easy*
- *French Riviera Made Easy*
- *Italy Made Easy*
- *Oslo Made Easy*
- *Paris Made Easy*
- *Paris Walks*
- *Provence Made Easy*

For a list of all Europe Made Easy travel guides, and to purchase our books, visit www.eatndrink.com

Made in the USA
Middletown, DE
27 November 2019

79581232R00086